D0955803

PRAISE FOR *WEALTH MADE EASY*

"Greg has made connections and gathered wealth creation advice from some of the world's mega-money individuals. Follow his advice and watch what happens. Bingo! You win."
—*Bob Proctor, author of* The ABCs of Success

"Great book. I recommend it highly."
—*David Meltzer, founder of Sports 1 Marketing*

"If we do not learn from others, how are we to learn? *Wealth Made Easy* is your answer."
—*Don Green, CEO of the Napoleon Hill Foundation*

"Greg Reid has upped his game with this treasure trove of hacks with which we can learn and apply. I've been underlining nonstop. This is the real deal."
—*David M. Corbin, author of* Preventing BrandSlaughter

"Each page is filled with golden nuggets of prosperity."
—*Dr. Frank Shankwitz, creator and a founder of the Make-A-Wish Foundation*

WEALTH
MADE EASY

WEALTH MADE EASY

Millionaires and Billionaires
Help You Crack the Code
to Getting Rich

DR. GREG REID

with Gary M. Krebs

BenBella Books, Inc.
Dallas, TX

BenBella Books, Inc.
10440 N. Central Expressway, Suite 800
Dallas, TX 75231
www.benbellabooks.com
Send feedback to feedback@benbellabooks.com

Printed in the United States of America
10 9 8 7 6 5 4 3 2 1

Library of Congress Cataloging-in-Publication Control Number: 2018055619.
ISBN 9781946885463
eISBN 9781948836180

Editing by Scott Calamar
Proofreading by Greg Teague and Amy Zarkos
Text design by Publishers' Design and Production Services, Inc.
Text composition by PerfecType, Nashville, TN
Cover design by Emily Weigel
Origami bull designed and folded by Travis Nolan, AdroitOrigami.com
Cover photos by Sarah Avinger (origami) and © Shutterstock / ivangal (line art)
Printed by Lake Book Manufacturing

Distributed to the trade by Two Rivers Distribution, an Ingram brand
www.tworiversdistribution.com

Special discounts for bulk sales (minimum of 25 copies) are available. Please contact bulkorders@benbellabooks.com

To all of the entrepreneurs, small business owners, moguls, business professionals, and captains of industry who vow to take action and apply the great wealth of knowledge they are about to receive in this book.

Don't count the days. Make the days count.
— Muhammad Ali, heavyweight champion boxer, activist, and philanthropist

CONTENTS

PART TWO: MOGUL MINDSET

PART THREE: MAKING IT HAPPEN

PART FOUR: WINNING WISDOM

SHORTCUTS TO SUCCESS

We all love to take shortcuts. We'll do anything to shave a minute off our daily commutes, avoid slaving away for hours to prepare dinner, and shed pounds without sweating on a treadmill. We're always on the hunt to find the path of least resistance to achieve our goals.

This book is designed for impatient, driven people just like us.

IT'S OKAY TO CUT THE LINE

As children, we were punished for cutting in line. When we grew older and became more "responsible," we discovered that we were often rewarded for this same behavior at work—with raises, job promotions, and elaborate award presentations in front of our peers.

Wealth Made Easy—the book you are holding in your hands—is your free pass to cut the line and achieve financial prosperity. But no one is going to berate you for skipping a few steps to get there. If anything, they'll think you're cunning and clever and wish they'd figured it out first.

We've seen the word "hack" crop up a lot lately—not always as a positive. Computer hacking has received a great deal of coverage, causing concern and outright panic both for businesses (as in cases of data breaches involving customer information) and for governments (as in foreign interference with elections, like the 2016 Russian cyberattack on the DNC).

On the other hand, so-called "life hacks" have been made widely available in books and in YouTube videos. These are commonsense ways to manage tasks in a simpler, more efficient manner. An example would be tying a colorful ribbon on a suitcase when traveling so it is easily recognizable on the baggage-claim conveyor belt and won't get taken by someone else by mistake.

This book is a collection of "wealth hacks," an unprecedentedly valuable type of shortcut that we've made easy for anyone to follow and implement. The millionaires and billionaires who contributed their knowledge to this book have never shared their secrets anywhere else, and certainly such a body of prized moneymaking advice has never before been collected in any one place. Together we'll witness and break down the principles behind what these millionaires and billionaires did to get ridiculously rich—even though they likely didn't consider them "hacks" when they first conceived them.

SEEK COUNSEL, NOT OPINIONS

Everybody needs some level of help and encouragement when they start out—even those who manage to skip a few steps. Don

Green, CEO of the Napoleon Hill Foundation, recommends that you, "Seek the counsel of those who have expertise outside their own."

Mr. Green was being specific with his choice of the word "counsel" rather than "opinions." What he means is that if you need help and expert advice to build wealth, don't rely on people offering opinions because that's all they'll give: opinions. Those aren't facts. Friends and family will pooh-pooh your concept out of hand and say it's a "bad idea" because they are ignorant on the subject; they think they're helping you by being hypercritical.

As recounted in *Three Feet from Gold* (by Sharon L. Lechter and the author*), this is like a family member who doesn't write and who hasn't read a book in years telling a wannabe novelist friend, "Don't bother, you're crazy—no one ever really makes it." Little do these well-intentioned people realize that they are bursting your creative bubble and shattering your dreams without a shred of knowledge to back up their pessimism.

When you obtain counsel, however, it means you're going to the wisest, most experienced, most clever people on the planet in that specific area. These are people who paid their dues and climbed—if not clawed—their way to the top. In the example of becoming a published novelist, expert counsel might mean conferring one-on-one with a best-selling author, a literary agent, or an editor at a major publishing house.

You've probably been asking yourself: *How can I learn from the super wealthy when they don't seem willing to share, and I don't have access to them anyway?*

---

*Throughout the book "the author" refers to Dr. Greg Reid.

The ultra rich may have been passing their moneymaking techniques and wisdom along to their inner tribes and to subsequent generations of family, but they have been clutching them tight and not sharing them with the masses. Simply put, the rich have kept their time-tested expertise to themselves; many even took their secrets with them to their graves.

Wealth Made Easy puts their expert counsel right at your fingertips. You don't have to hunt down the super successful, which would be impossible for most people. All you need to do is turn the pages. Although it's highly doubtful every one of these brilliant individuals is in your direct area of business interest, we've made sure that all of the wealth hacks included are general enough to apply to pretty much every field of endeavor.

Expert counsel is by no means a "get rich" scheme. Within these pages are *the actual techniques millionaires and billionaires used to make their self-perpetuating fortunes*. We're going to hack into their minds and extract their secret sauces, pinpointing the exact strategies they used to create a life of sustained abundance.

HOW TO CRACK "THE CODE" OF THE SUPER WEALTHY

The innovative and brilliant minds who share their strategies in these pages come from a wide range of diverse businesses, but all have one thing in common: astronomical net worth. As you'll see just up ahead, they range in ages and areas of expertise, from established long-standing business people to young, innovative entrepreneurs—each with their own take on success. Our more than three dozen contributors offer mastery from the bottom of the sea to outer space: CEOs and business executives from the construction, energy, and automotive industries; investors and entrepreneurs; inventors and innovators of games, products, websites, online businesses, and medical and dental devices; motivational speakers and authors; TV hosts, directors, and producers; media magnates; and real estate developers.

Among the elite super wealthy, there exists something we'll refer to as the "high net worth code." "High net worth" are individuals who have over one million dollars in liquid assets. We're going to gain access to the *code*—or never revealed secret—from each amazing high net worth person included in this book; we'll simplify and then translate it for practical use. We'll dive deep as we hack into their moneymaking techniques.

Not only are you going to find out *what* these wealthy people did, but also *how* they did it. We've distilled their concepts into easily comprehensible, actionable steps that can be applied to pretty much any type of business you might wish to enter or expand.

This book is simply written and designed so you'll have an *aha!* moment not only on every page, but also in each and every paragraph. We've divided the hacks into convenient thematic parts (although some could potentially fit into more than one category):

- **Big Ideas (Part One):** This is another way of saying *innovation* or the creative things that will drive your entrepreneurial efforts into the stratosphere.

- **Mogul Mindset (Part Two):** This section contains Wealth Hacks designed to guide your *attitude* to help you achieve unparalleled success.
- **Making It Happen (Part Three):** Here you'll find *strategic* hacks—the things that will help you execute your Big Ideas.
- **Winning Wisdom (Part Four):** These are timeless *street-savvy* gold nuggets.

You can read this book front to back, in chunks by section, or in whatever fashion you most prefer for browsing. As stated in Wealth Hack #66, it doesn't matter how you ingest your vitamins—as long as they get into your system. The intent is that you can pull out the book now (or even twenty years from now), turn to any page, and you will pick up an invaluable tip or inspiring words that keep you motivated on your lifelong mission to build wealth.

A FEW IMPORTANT WORDS
FROM NAPOLEON HILL

Napoleon Hill begins his 1937 masterwork, *Think and Grow Rich*, with this mind-blowing sentence that continues to resonate all these years later: "Today will be one of the most important days of your life."

Hill's book remains a business bible, but times have changed. While, generally, the basic principles of business, success, and accumulating wealth still share an underlying foundation, the world is very different than it was eighty years ago—there are different techniques, different strategies. In that time we've gone from newspaper and radio advertising to the power of the internet, to devices that people carry in their pockets and refer to constantly. The way people communicate and network has transformed society and interpersonal relationships.

In the pages that follow, we build on the success of Hill's advice. With this book in hand, you have another important day to add to your list: The day you start *hacking away* at your dreams of success. That day needs to be *today*. Right now.

Let's start cutting the line.

WHO ARE THE
WEALTH HACKERS?

The "Wealth Hackers" whose counsel is featured in this book are a mastermind group of super wealthy people who are sharing their proven success nuggets with you. Sometimes the hacks are from one specific individual, sometimes from the author, and sometimes from the collective group.

You may think to yourself, *Some of these hacks seem so obvious, why isn't everyone already using them?*

That is precisely the genius of the Wealth Hackers I spoke to: They often found their respective gold mines hidden in plain sight through just one boiled-down secret—and then acted on it. The insider hacks in this book are therefore often deceptively brilliant in their simplicity and straightforwardness.

What does this mean? In short, that anyone can use these hacks—including YOU!

WITHOUT FURTHER ADO:

Here are the illustrious Wealth Hackers—all have made millions, some even billions—who contributed one or more revelations based on their respective experiences, expertise, and successes.

ERNESTO ANCIRA, JR.: Chairman, president, and chief executive officer at Ancira-Winton Chevrolet, Inc., which has thirteen dealerships based in San Antonio, Texas, and annual revenue of more than $1 billion.

ROB (ROBERT) ANGEL: Game inventor who created the enormously popular guessing game Pictionary.

LES (LESLIE CALVIN) BROWN: One of the world's most renowned motivational speakers, Brown has coached and consulted with Fortune 500 CEOs, small business owners, and nonprofit and community leaders from all sectors of society. He has written a number of best-selling books and audiobooks.

CRAIG CLEMENS: Lauded ad copywriter, who brought in $1 billion in sales, turned cofounder of Golden Hippo Media.

DR. DWIGHT DAMON: Industry-leading orthodontist widely known for his development of the innovative Damon System. Dr. Damon is a pioneer in the field, lecturing worldwide to both doctors and staff on the most advanced orthodontic treatment philosophies.

SCOTT DUFFY: TV/online host, keynote speaker, and business-growth expert. He began his career working for best-selling author and speaker Tony Robbins and went on to work for several big media brands such as CBS Sportsline, NBC Internet, and FOXSports.com.

MARSHALL EZRALOW: Founder of the Ezralow Company, one of the largest and most successful real estate development companies in California and perhaps the United States. This fourth-generation family business has redefined the landscape of Southern California real estate with its acquisition, development, and management of more than 20,000 apartments and six million square feet of business space.

JOSH FLAGG: Real estate agent and host of the Bravo TV series *Million Dollar Listing Los Angeles*. Flagg has sold more than $1 billion worth of property, is a top-ten real estate agent in Los Angeles, and has become the number-one volume agent and the number-two agent in sales in the area.

DAN FLEYSHMAN: The youngest founder of a publicly traded company in history at age twenty-three. Mr. Fleyshman launched the Who's Your Daddy energy drink into 55,000 retail stores and military bases. He went on to launch Victory Poker in 2010, building the third-largest team of professional players out of the 550 poker sites on the market. Mr. Fleyshman is an active angel investor and advisor to more than 24 businesses that range from mobile apps and tech companies to successful monthly box subscription sites such as Dollar Beard Club and consumer products like Uwheels—both of which exceeded $5 million in sales in less than eight months.

JEFF FRIED: President and chief energizing officer of All In Entertainment, LLC, a Washington, DC–based firm representing sports and media interests, the promotion of worldwide Championship Boxing, and other entertainment events.

PHIL (PHILLIP B.) GOLDFINE: Los Angeles–based producer and founder of Hollywood Media Bridge. Goldfine has sixty film credits, including *A Christmas Story* 2, and has worked on five television series. He was executive producer for the 2014 documentary *The Lady in Number 6: Music Saved My Life*, which was awarded the Oscar for Best Documentary Short Subject. His TV credits include *Lawman* (A&E) and the Emmy-nominated film *Seal Team Six* (National Geographic).

RON (RONALD L.) GRAHAM: Retired president, CEO, and (later) chairman of the board of The Graham Group, one of Canada's leading construction companies with revenues exceeding $1.8 billion annually. Graham is recognized as one of Canada's fifty best employers as well as one of the country's fifty best-managed companies.

JULES HAIMOVITZ: Chairman of the board and chief executive officer at Global Entertainment & Media Holdings Corporation. At Metro Goldwyn Mayer Inc., he served as president of MGM Networks Inc., executive consultant to the CEO, and chair of the library task force. He was also president and chief operating officer of Spelling Entertainment Inc. and held senior positions at Viacom Inc., King World Productions, Inc., ITC Entertainment Group, and Dick Clark Productions, Inc. Mr. Haimovitz is perhaps best known for having started up the Showtime, Lifetime, Sundance, and Smithsonian cable channels and for having acquired companies such as MTV Networks.

NIK HALIK: Angel investor and 5 Day Weekend Strategist who amassed substantial wealth through savvy investments in property, business, and the financial markets. Mr. Halik's companies have financially educated and life coached more than one million clients in more than fifty-seven countries. Mr. Halik is also a stakeholder in a number of businesses around the world, including Vertex Media, a Hollywood television and film production company, and Poptik, a patented Sub Optic print technology.

KEVIN HARRINGTON: American entrepreneur and business executive, Mr. Harrington is the founder of As Seen on TV. He has appeared on the TV series *Shark Tank*.

JEFFREY HAYZLETT: Prime-time television host of *C-Suite with Jeffrey Hayzlett* and *Executive Perspectives* on C-Suite TV and the host of the award-winning *All Business with Jeffrey Hayzlett* on C-Suite Radio. He is a Hall of Fame speaker, best-selling author, and chairman of C-Suite Network.

WAYNE H. HENUSET: Co-owner, cochairman, and president of Energy Alberta Corporation and president of Willow

Park Wines & Spirits—the largest privately owned liquor store in Canada. He is a longstanding member of the oil and gas business community and has owned and run various car dealerships, among other highly successful business ventures.

JEFF (JEFFREY D.) HOFFMAN: Accomplished entrepreneur and innovator best known as a founding executive team member of Priceline.com. Mr. Hoffman has established a long and winning track record in the fields of online auction and retail, software, and entertainment. He is currently chief executive officer at Enable Holdings, Inc. (formerly uBid.com Holdings, Inc.) of uBid, Inc. He previously served as the chief executive officer and founding partner of Virtual Shopping, Inc.

NAVEEN JAIN: Business executive, entrepreneur, and the founder and CEO of Viome Inc. Previously, he was founder and CEO of InfoSpace and cofounder of Moon Express.

GAVIN KEILLY: Founder of GBK Productions, which organizes special events for the entertainment industry and the nonprofit sector.

RON KLEIN: Dubbed "the Grandfather of Possibilities," Klein is best known as the inventor of the magnetic strip on the credit card. He is also the creator of the credit card validity checking system and the developer of computerized systems for real estate Multiple Listing Services (MLS), voice response for the banking industry, and bond quotation and trade information for the New York Stock Exchange. He is the founder and CEO of Technitrend, Inc. and General Associates, Inc.

C. REED KNIGHT, JR.: Founder of Knight's Armament Company, a premier weapons manufacturer offering complete weapon systems, modular accessories, and Knight-Vision electro-optics.

TONINO LAMBORGHINI: Founder of the Tonino Lamborghini company, renowned for such branded luxury design products as watches, eyewear, smartphones, perfumes, furniture, clothing, sports accessories, signature beverages, five-star boutique hotels, lounges, and restaurants. Mr. Lamborghini is the son of Ferruccio Lamborghini—creator of the world famous Lamborghini sports cars—and heir to the Lamborghini fortune.

DR. GENE N. LANDRUM: Creator of the Chuck E. Cheese's concept of family entertainment. Dr. Landrum has written numerous books, and he lectures extensively.

JEFF LEVITAN: Business leader, entrepreneur, success coach, and executive chairman of the World Financial Group (WFG).

WALTER O'BRIEN: Irish businessman and founder of Scorpion Computer Services, Inc. He is best known as executive producer and writer of the *Scorpion* TV series.

CRAIG SHAH: Global CEO and cofounder of Craig Shelly fine watches and jewelry.

BRIAN SIDORSKY: Founder and CEO of Lansdowne Equity Ventures Ltd., a highly profitable family-owned real estate business, with operations in land banking—the practice of buying land with the purpose of reselling it at a future date at a higher price—and real estate development. Mr. Sidorsky built southern Alberta's largest independent furniture and appliance store.

STEVE SIMS: Founder of Bluefish, a luxury concierge service.

BRIAN SMITH: Founder of UGG boots, innovator, keynote speaker, and author.

DAN (DANIEL) SMITH: Founder and president of Energy Capital Fund. Smith, a trained chemical engineer and authority in oil and gas development, also served critical roles at Sonat Exploration and XTO Energy.

ROB SNYDER: Founder of Stream Energy, a Dallas-based provider of energy, wireless, protective, and home services.

MARC STANILOFF: Chief executive officer, president, and chairman of Superior Lodging Corp. Mr. Staniloff had been instrumental in the development of 110 Super 8 motels and Wingate Inns in Canada from 1993 to 2007.

GREG (GREGORY P.) STEMM: Cofounder and chief executive officer of Odyssey Marine Exploration, Inc., a pioneer in the exploration and archaeological excavation of deep-ocean shipwrecks. Mr. Stemm has played an important role in the development of new technologies and private-sector standards for underwater cultural heritage resource management. Mr. Stemm's first major deep-ocean project was the *Tortugas*, a colonial Spanish shipwreck that was the world's first complete remote robotic archaeological excavation.

TOMMY TALLARICO: Musician and video game music composer who is best known as the cocreator of the concert series Video Games Live. He has worked on more than three hundred video games since the 1980s.

STEPHEN VAN DEVENTER: Chairman and chief executive officer at Preveceutical Medical Inc. Mr. Van Deventer is an entrepreneur and owner of Cornerstone Global Partners Inc.

ANSON WILLIAMS: Actor, director, singer, entrepreneur, and inventor best known for his role as Potsie on the *Happy Days* TV show. He has directed episodes of TV's *The Secret Life of the American Teenager*; *Lizzie McGuire*; *Baywatch*; *Beverly Hills, 90210*; *Melrose Place*; and *Star Trek: Voyager*; among others. Williams has patented several inventions and, motivated by a near-fatal crash and his uncle, Dr. Henry Heimlich (creator of the Heimlich maneuver), developed Alert Drops as a stimulant for sleepy drivers.

KEVIN YOUNG: Innovator, visionary, consultant, and investor. Presently, he is vice president, corporate development, at Medicus Global, LLC. He is best known as a codeveloper of the first prepaid phone card platform and distribution company in the United States.

Part One

Big Ideas

WEALTH HACK #1

Buy dirt.

TIME + DIRT = WEALTH.

Canadian land mogul Brian Sidorsky shares a concept so powerful and easy to understand that it challenges your imagination.

When asked how he amassed a huge fortune in raw, undeveloped land, he sat back in his chair and grinned.

"Time plus dirt is wealth!" he exclaimed.

Sidorsky clarifies his concept as follows: "Find a town, anywhere in North America that is growing 20 to 25 percent a year. Pinpoint their 'Main Street' and draw a line out eight miles from that location and buy that land. That is the 'dirt.' Rent the soil to local farmers who will pay the rent that covers the costs so it's free—not to mention, you get great vegetables. As the town continues to expand, eventually it ends up on your property where you own the largest lot and, since you are already near

Main Street, you can then sell that land to a big box store for one hundred times what you paid for it."

` *Boom!*

The major fortunes in America have been made in land.
        —John D. Rockefeller, oil magnate and industrialist

WEALTH HACK #2

*Create a product, good, or service that people
will happily spend all of their savings to obtain.*

People don't save up all their money to buy things like scented
candles or picture frames. However, they will save their
entire fortunes to buy a Lamborghini luxury vehicle.

Leveraging his family's world-renowned brand name, Tonino
Lamborghini opened up nightclubs and world-class resorts with
the concept that people will eagerly spend their hard-earned
cash to have the best experience of their lives.

You wouldn't spend a thousand dollars to stay in your own
home, yet you would happily hand over that amount to experience the benefits of a world-class luxury hotel *just once*. You
would automatically associate the Lamborghini brand name
with *luxury* and be more than willing to splurge on staying at
one of their resorts, knowing that your high expectations and
gratification will be met.

Disney resorts also create that same level of perceived value
through their branding. Customers desire the experience so

much that they are eagerly willing to save up their hard-earned paychecks to vacation there.

Go over the top with what you offer to your customers like Lamborghini, Disney, and even certain universities, such as Harvard. If you can create a luxury "Lamborghini" product, good, or service in your industry, you will have discovered the secret to sustained abundance.

I don't design clothes, I design dreams.
—Ralph Lauren, fashion designer

WEALTH HACK #3

*Info-sponge—bring ideas from outside
your industry into your business.*

A BROWNING BANANA =
AN EMPTY AIRPLANE SEAT = $$.

Say what?

Billionaire Jeff Hoffman watches trends and connects unrelated puzzle pieces over time that suddenly fit together as if they were always meant to be. He matches things like a browning banana with an empty airplane seat and makes a fortune.

Jeff refers to this as "info-sponging." You can find him in front of a newsstand perusing trade magazines covering other industries for ideas that he can adapt for his own business.

During one of these ten-minute sessions, Jeff found an article on how to handle distressed inventory.

Now, if you're in the business of manufacturing, selling, and warehousing products, distressed inventory is the bane of your existence. It means no one purchased what you had to sell, and the product is likely to be wasting away (i.e., browning bananas). Distressed inventory never returns once it's lost.

Years ago, supermarket chains either tossed their distressed inventory or donated it to food banks. Entrepreneurs saw dollar signs and created "salvage grocery stores" to buy these damaged items cheaply and then resell them right away before the clock ran out. It's win-win all around.

Jeff had a lightning flash: What if he were to create a virtual salvage grocery store—but for unsold airline seats?

From a financial standpoint, an unsold airplane seat is no different from that browning banana. Once the airplane takes off, the value of that seat is worthless.

Cake and Ice Cream with a Twist

There is no limit to the info-sponging concept. It can work with an endless variety of ideas that have been mixed and matched.

Here is an old one invented by confectioner Harry Burt:

Ice cream + Stick = Good Humor ice cream.

This is a newer one with the same twist:

Cake + Stick = Cake Pop (and now virtually every bakery seems to offer cake pops).

Info-sponge!

This is how Priceline.com—now a $70.5 billion business—was conceived. Priceline treats unsold airline seats as if they are distressed inventory, selling them at cheaper fares as the takeoffs become imminent. It's another win-win for everyone—and, for Jeff Hoffman, ten minutes at a newsstand that were well spent.

Innovation is taking two things that already exist and putting them together in a new way.
            —Tom Freston, entertainment executive

WEALTH HACK #4

Build wealth by helping people.

Here's a fact:

HELPING PEOPLE = MEGA $$.

That's not as crazy as it sounds. Many wealthy people understand that in order to make tons of money, you have to do some good and give back.

I'm not talking about charity (although that's perfectly fine, of course). I'm referring to creating a product or service—or investing in one—that solves a problem and makes a real difference in improving people's lives.

That may sound corny. But let's take a look at rich inventor Dr. Dwight Damon.

He recognized that *everyone hated braces*. They hurt like hell. The wires were tight and cut into the gums. They were hard to clean. They also looked pretty terrible ("railroad tracks") while being latched onto kids' teeth right smack in the middle of puberty.

Let's face it: *Braces totally sucked.*

Dr. Damon didn't understand why the industry used orthodontics that applied seven hundred times more pressure on teeth than was necessary. He used his expert skills with machinery to design braces that were more comfortable, less visible, and required less wear time.

He made a fortune on helping people improve their smiles while at the same time enabling millions of kids to get through it without nearly as much pain and suffering. Since then, he's filed 20,000 patents, which have helped millions of people worldwide.

One simple tweak can truly put a smile on your face.

To do more for the world than the world does for you,
that is success.

> —Henry Ford, founder of the Ford Motor Company

WEALTH HACK #5

Find a need and fill it.

How does C. Reed Knight, Jr., owner of Knight's Armament, make a billion dollars in weapons manufacturing?

He listens to his clients and gives them exactly what they ask for.

As Reed describes, "I asked the military, 'What is your biggest challenge?' They answered, 'We can't hit our targets at night. It's too dark and we just can't see them.'"

"'Well,' we proposed, 'what if we used the same technology as the night-vision goggles to make a scope to help the soldiers see at night?'"

Sure enough, the military tested them out and they worked— so well, in fact, that the military offered the scopes to *all* their divisions.

By giving the clients exactly what they wanted and solving their challenge, Knight's Armament created a product that became an essential tool that everyone needed to have.

It is so important to experience what your customers are experiencing and listen to their suggestions.
      —David Neeleman, entrepreneur and founder of four
major airlines, including JetBlue Airways

WEALTH HACK #6

Lead the receiver.

In the last Wealth Hack, Reed Knight, Jr., explained how listening to customers and anticipating their needs drives his business. As you'll discover here, it's possible to anticipate a major opportunity without a customer even being part of the equation. All you need to do is keep your eyes open downfield and think and react like an NFL quarterback. Hang in there with this analogy, all will be revealed . . .

There's a company in Canada—Superior Lodging Corp.—that spent $72 million to build extended-stay luxury-suite resorts in a desolate, empty field.

Was CEO Marc Staniloff crazy? Why spend such an enormous amount of money to build a resort in the middle of nowhere?

The answer was found in a location near the field, where you could see a construction site filled with all kinds of bulldozers, forklifts, excavators, and dump trucks.

What was being built there? The greatest long-term health-care facility in all of Canada.

Staniloff recognized that the executives affiliated with the health-care facility would need a place to stay—and there was nothing else around. More important, he projected even further outward and realized that, once the facility was completed, recovering patients—as well as their visiting families and friends—would also be looking for lodging.

The Mouse That Didn't Roar—At First

Any time you feel impatient about your product or service taking too long to make money, keep in mind one name: Douglas Engelbart.

Who?

Engelbart should be way up there with Bill Gates and Steve Jobs in the pantheon of technogeniuses. Yet few people know his name or his major contribution to computing: the invention of the mouse.

Believe it or not, the computer mouse was first patented in 1970. Engelbart's invention—originally dubbed the "X-Y Position Indicator for a Display System" but then changed to the cuter word "mouse" because Engelbart thought the wire in the back looked like a rodent's tail— was way ahead of its time, and it took decades for the technology to catch up.

The lesson? Stick by your mouse, whatever it may be— you never know when the market might suddenly be ready for it.

In football, the quarterback never throws the ball where the wide receiver is standing. He throws it downfield and allows the receiver to catch up to it.

Touchdown!

Find the need and then fill it.

—Anonymous

WEALTH HACK #7

Simplify everything.

Some of the most brilliant and most useful business inventions weren't as basic as "finding a need and filling it." It's possible to question why an accepted process takes ten or twelve steps when it could be condensed into just one and save people a lot of time and effort. Some of these solutions are "invisible in plain sight," which means it requires ingenuity and resourcefulness to capitalize on them. In other words, one must develop the ability to notice where things can be *simplified*.

Years ago, when people used a credit card, the cashier had to look up and verify each and every customer's number in a giant book. It used to mean scores of people had to wait hours on line in stores until this laborious task was completed. Can you imagine that happening now?

Today, you just whip out your card and it's a lightning-fast swipe in the machine. (Or, if you have a chip, you slide the card in.)

None of this would have been possible if Ron Klein hadn't simplified things and invented the reading validation system for the magnetic strip on credit cards. Klein noticed that the cashier lines in Macy's department store were way too long because of the time it took to look up all of these credit card numbers. His goal was to add value by saving steps in this ridiculous process, which no one else had the presence of mind to question.

Klein, one of the great problem-solvers, invented a device that could mimic a reel-to-reel tape machine and copy numbers onto magnetic tape. In fact, he was the first person to make "humans a machine." He did this by having the customer slide the card through a device at the right pace that would enable it to pick up the numbers and verify the account on the spot.

These inventions—the magnetic strip on the credit card and the credit card validity checking system—also shifted the onus from the stores to the credit card companies to produce cards that could be scanned. They saved a ton of time for retailers and customers, dramatically cutting down the length of the cashier lines.

Now *that* is simplifying a problem.

A great problem-solver is usually open to new ideas,
innately curious, and good at working with others.
                    —Richard Branson, entrepreneur, investor, author,
                              philanthropist, founder of the Virgin Group

WEALTH HACK #8

*Combine unrelated business ideas
and make them your own.*

Gene Landrum did something seemingly impossible when he founded Chuck E. Cheese's. He created an entirely new business model by combining several different ideas into one chain: food, family, and amusement park–type entertainment.

Food: Kids love pizza.

Amusement park–type entertainment: Kids love things like video games, whack-a-mole, and air hockey.

Combine pizza and amusement park entertainment and you have happy kids *and* happy parents. Why parents? Because they can sit at the table, take a breather, and eat while their kids are busy playing in the gaming area.

The hybrid pizza chain/entertainment center concept was revolutionary and broke the mold of old thinking that had kept dining and kids' entertainment separate. Bookstores that have coffee bars are working a similar idea.

What businesses can you combine to create something entirely new?

Wisdom from Dr. Gene Landrum

Dr. Gene Landrum is a sage who is loaded with pearls of wisdom. Here are just a few quick ones on some of the famous people he believes every entrepreneur should strive to emulate.

Be a titan like Alexander the Great.
Be arrogant like architect Frank Lloyd Wright.
Be mystical like fashion designer Coco Chanel.
Be gutsy like FedEx founder Fred Smith.
Follow your bliss like mythologist Joseph Campbell.

You can't learn new stuff unless you're willing to go down strange roads.

—Gene Landrum, founder of Chuck E. Cheese's

WEALTH HACK #9

Double up and triple up.

Remember prepaid phone cards? They took place in the years BCP (Before Cell Phones), also known as BMP (Before Mobile Phones). Take your pick of which acronym you prefer.

When you received a prepaid phone card, you could make as many phone calls as you wanted, up to the value of the card using a special number printed on it. During the BCP years, this had great value for business travelers, commuters, college kids, and anyone using a pay phone (remember those)?

Kevin Young, who codeveloped the first prepaid phone card platform and distribution company in the United States, made a killing on these cards. It was a brilliant business model: You could turn one minute of phone time into a guaranteed dollar while doing hardly anything except providing the card and a marginal payment to the phone company. It didn't involve any billing, and costs for manufacturing and shipping were minimal.

That's not the half of the profit. Kevin realized it was time to *double up.*

The *real* money wasn't in the cards per se, but in the ability to adapt them using icons and special brands as premium opportunities with business partners. The card was the reward for doing business and being a good customer. Kevin didn't mind that his company was second banana to the main product being offered because he made lots of money doing nothing. These are just a few examples of premiums:

- Buy a Disney vacation and get a prepaid phone card— with Mickey Mouse on it, of course.
- Buy a tin of Folgers coffee and get a free prepaid card.
- Buy a Happy Meal at McDonald's and get a free prepaid card.
- Buy a large pack of Post-it Notes with a free prepaid phone card inside.

In each case: What a deal!

You get the point with the above examples. The "free add-on" concept was so adaptable, it was applied to just about anything and everything. People felt they were getting something valuable for nothing.

Soon enough there were even Elvis and JFK cards, which turned into valuable collectibles after usage. As if that wasn't enough, the concept of prepaid phone cards became so accepted and widely trusted that they became a charitable vehicle as well in many cases, such as for Habitat for Humanity with Jimmy Carter. The organization would cover the expense of branding on the card, and the end user (the customer purchasing the card) would pay face value for it, a portion of which would go back to the charity.

Brainstorm the Next Vehicle for Premiums

Premiums, gifts, and complimentary giveaways have been around for a long time. Companies have been placing little toy surprises in Cracker Jack boxes for decades. Moisturizer and perfume samples have been inside magazines for many years.

Think about how the digital world has revolutionized the art of the premium for customers. Now it's as simple as going to a website and downloading an app with a bar code to scan. Although paper coupons still exist—and I'm sure many grandmothers still spend their Sundays clipping them—companies like Groupon have made a killing connecting customers and businesses by offering discounts and add-ons with purchase.

This type of exchange has come a long way in a short period of time due to massive disruptive technology—from the creation of the internet to the invention of wireless capability to the ability of businesses to offer individual codes to customers that may be scanned by vendors. In other words, game changers in the way we conduct business with consumers. Before considering how you will market your company's product or service, think about what the next disruption might be and how you can take advantage of it.

Remember: Don't be afraid to give away a free sample before the customer makes a decision.

This last one is actually a *triple wealth hack*:

HABITAT FOR HUMANITY PREPAID CARD = REVENUE + CHARITY + COLLECTIBLE.

The beautiful part of this is that if the card ended up lost or unused, the sales had already been made and the spread was pure profit minus the charitable donation and the cost of the phone time.

Try to come up with a prepaid business model that involves revenue, charity, and collectible aspects, and you are guaranteed to have a winner.

> *Groupon as a company—it's built into the business model—is about surprise. A new deal that surprises you every day.*
> —Andrew Mason, founder and former CEO of Groupon

WEALTH HACK #10

Seek areas of deregulation.

L et's shove aside all political views for a moment and look at just one thing:

Business opportunity. What is the market's best friend that leads to immediate and unbridled business opportunity?

Deregulation.

You probably already know this but I'll state it anyway: *Regulation* is when the government clamps down on businesses by creating restrictions intended to help protect the people from an identified hazard (i.e., environmental issues). *Deregulation* is when those burdens to the companies go away, allowing them to produce and distribute as they see fit.

Rob Snyder, the founder of Stream Energy—a Dallas-based provider of energy, wireless, protective, and home services—has always looked for areas that were not regulated. Now, with deregulation happening across the spectrum in the United States, this tactic can be especially lucrative.

When the government is about to let go of its grip, make sure you are the first in line.

Know What You Need to Know—And What You Don't Need to Know

The old way of thinking: Only invest in what you know and understand.

The new way of thinking: You don't need to know everything about your investment (unless you are buying and selling real estate).

A prime example of the above is blockchain. You can buy, sell, and trade things anonymously without the need of a bank. You don't need to know everything about Bitcoins in order to make a lot of coin!

Energy deregulation will be the largest transfer of wealth in history.

—Warren Buffett, investor and chairman and CEO of Berkshire Hathaway

WEALTH HACK #11

State it and create it.

When it comes to entrepreneurial success, this couldn't be more true—whether it's launching a cable channel, developing a new app, or even opening a sushi restaurant.

What do you need for this field of dreams to really happen? Three things:

1. A really good idea
2. Perfect execution
3. Knowledge of what the customer wants before he or she does

The above three criteria are how entertainment executive Jules Haimovitz built several fields of dreams on cable TV, including the Showtime, Lifetime, Sundance, and Smithsonian cable channels. "Showtime started out as just a good idea," he describes. "We never thought about wealth, we just did it right . . . We created something where we knew a market was waiting for us. We simply had to build a medium in order to give it to them."

If you have a really good idea for a product or business: visualize it, write it down, map it out, and head right to the shed to start building.

> *If you build it, they will come.*
> —from the film *Field of Dreams*

WEALTH HACK #12

To be great, authenticate.

G reg Stemm has one of the coolest jobs on the planet. As
cofounder and chief executive officer of Odyssey Marine
Exploration, Inc., he explores and excavates deep-ocean shipwrecks. His team has made some of the most important underwater finds in history: the SS *Republic*, the HMS *Victory*, the
SS *Gairsoppa*, the SS *Central America*, *Black Swan*, *Tortugas*,
and many others.

This guy is like Indiana Jones and Jacques Cousteau rolled
into one.

We're not going to get into the international political and
legal controversies of what happens with the treasures hauled
in by Greg and his team (i.e., who gets to own all this amazing
stuff). Suffice it to say, Greg is able to retain a fair share, and
he does donate a certain amount of every finding to the country
of origin (assuming it still exists) and often finds housing for
artifacts in proper museums.

Now you're wondering: What does Greg do with all of
the riches he gets to keep? He sells much of it, of course, at

significant profit. But the genius of his business model is how he distributes all of those old gold coins he finds at the bottom of the ocean.

Where and How Can You Add Perceived Value?

Pillows have been around a long time—perhaps as far back as Mesopotamia in 7000 BCE. They are now universally on every bed used by anyone who can afford them. You can find pillows in pretty much any kind of store from Macy's to Bed Bath & Beyond.

And yet, a guy named Mike Lindell has created a phenomenon with—guess what? MyPillow! Sure, it's a fantastic product—but how did the product command such attention?

Simple: Lindell added *perceived value*. He realized that his problems, neck and back pain, were caused by his flat pillow. And, wouldn't you know it: he found out that millions of other people were just as frustrated by their flat pillows as he was. This is how he created MyPillow—a pillow that doesn't go flat and prevents neck and back pain. What a wonderful promise for such a small investment!

Even in a crowded industry, there is always a way to find a wedge and build a distinctive brand. What you need to do is identify a problem with a commonly used product and then *solve it better than the competition*.

If you can accomplish this, rest assured you'll be sleeping comfortably in the lap of luxury in no time.

Let's say Greg discovers a huge chest containing half a million genuine seventeenth-century Spanish coins. He could sell them all off—but why miss out on a much bigger opportunity?

Greg won't just offer a coin to a collector or buff for a couple of bucks apiece. He creates a special certificate of authenticity to go along with the coin, verifying which wreck it came from and when it was discovered. In doing so, he has greatly *increased the perceived value of the coin*. Since he is the only one who has such a special, unique item to offer, he can sell the coin for twenty dollars.

Now do the math. Half a million coins times twenty dollars equals ten million dollars. That's a lot of booty!

Margin is a customer concept.
> —Paul Singer, hedge fund manager and founder of
> Elliott Management Corporation

WEALTH HACK #13

Capitalize on something unused.

When cable TV was just starting out, Kevin Harrington—later known for his role as one of the original "sharks" on the *Shark Tank* TV show—was among one of the early adopters who suddenly went from having four or five channels to thirty. He was told he would have all of these channels 24/7 and started binge watching at all hours of the day.

Then he noticed something. A few channels, such as the Discovery Channel, had no programming between the hours of 3 AM to 9 AM. The stations showed only colored bars. He called the cable company thinking he got rooked, but, as it turned out, some channels didn't have the budget for eighteen hours of programming. Six hours were left totally unused and wasted.

Harrington had a massive idea. He approached Discovery Channel and offered to fill up the six hours of empty airtime for only $1,000 a day. He created half-hour segments of product advertising and *voila!*—the infomercial (and "As Seen on TV") was born. He generated tens of millions of dollars from the exposure and, over the years, turned products like Ginsu,

Bowflex, Snuggie, and the ShamWow! into beloved household name brands.

The idea was translated to other networks, such as Lifetime, the Golf Channel, and the Home Shopping Network, which also went dark for a few hours in the early morning. The infomercials became so successful that the networks became anxious to sell Harrington airtime during regular day slots as well.

But wait—and there's more! Harrington bought unsold ("remnant") space in newspapers for products just before print time. He would get half-page ads at a 95 percent discount because he satisfied a need when the newspapers were desperate to fill space.

Look for the voids in your industry and then take advantage of them. Operators are standing by.

> *If you have that passion, it is conveyed through marketing. People see it. I get up before them and show them something new and wonderful. When I create something, I believe in it, and I am very passionate about it.*
>
> —Ron Pompeil, inventor and founder of Ronco

WEALTH HACK #14

Take advantage of obsolescence.

When machinery and other office equipment gets old, what do companies see?

Junk.

What do they do with the junk?

They donate it or toss it out.

Ron Klein does not see junk: He sees *opportunity*.

When Klein ran General Associates, Inc. (GA), he acquired large quantities of surplus Teletype equipment from the Western Union Company.

Why did he buy all of this worthless junk? The Teletype machine had become a relic.

Where others saw useless old junk, he saw beauty—and *money*—in obsolescence. Klein refurbished the old Teletype equipment and sold it to major communications companies. As a special service, GA converted many of them into special teleprinters for the hearing impaired with messages imprinted in Braille. He created a totally new and innovative use for what had been considered *junk*.

Old Is the New *New*

You never know when "old" will become "new." Ten years ago, who ever thought that vinyl records and turntables would be making a comeback? More than 7.6 million records sold in the first half of 2018 alone, according to Nielsen Music, which is a 19 percent increase over the same period the prior year. Sales of turntables have been steadily on the rise every year since 2012.

Think about what trends came and went—but might be returning due to a nostalgia craze. Who knows—maybe 8-track tapes will be the next to make a comeback!

Don't limit your imagination. Obsolescence can sometimes lead to amazing things. On Bleecker Street in New York City, there are jewelry designers who create cool rings, bracelets, and necklaces out of old *manual typewriter keys*.

What junk do you have lying around that can be converted into cash?

Obsolescence never meant the end of anything. It's just the beginning.

—Marshall McLuhan, professor,
philosopher, and media theorist

WEALTH HACK #15

Solve a ten-billion-dollar problem.

I f you are wondering why you haven't made ten billion dollars yet, perhaps it's because you haven't thought big enough. You probably haven't tried to solve a problem that impacts enough people on a grand enough scale. You haven't tried to solve a *ten-billion-dollar* problem.

Naveen Jain, the CEO of Viome, looks to solve problems that are universally shared, such as the root cause of major diseases. In essence, Viome seeks to expand human lifespans by asking the question: *What if illness could be elective?*

The company asserts that all disease is located in the gut. They provide home testing kits that are analyzed by a team of brilliant scientists. Customers get back a complete report on gut score, metabolic score, and body score. Based on these results—namely identifications of the microorganisms living in the gut—they can recommend a nutritional plan and supplements that can prevent diseases from surfacing.

Consider This Hot Tip

Biotech is one of the fastest-growing industries one can enter. Some sources expect biotech to reach as high as $727 billion by 2025. If you have a chance to start up or invest in such a company, you have the added benefit of helping people by being involved in research that can cure and prevent disease.

Of course, as with any investment, there can be significant risk. In the case of biotech, the results of drug trials can make or break a product. Savvy investors look for low-profile drugs with big promise (i.e., fighting off cancer) that are successfully moving into the *second phase* of testing rather than right out of the gate before the trials start. By waiting until the second phase, you may miss out on getting in on the first ground floor—but it doesn't matter because the product is under the radar and won't have many investors yet. The benefits are that you have lower financial risk than when it is untested and higher potential upside if it blows out.

As Naveen says, "If your gut is not at ease, you get disease." Now *that* is a ten-billion-dollar idea.

The Band-Aid is an inexpensive, convenient, and remarkably versatile solution to an astonishing array of problems.

> —Malcolm Gladwell, staff writer for *The New Yorker* and author of *Blink* and *The Tipping Point*

WEALTH HACK #16

Save lives.

In Wealth Hack #4, Dr. Dwight Damon explored how to make a difference in people's lives by improving their health and appearance through revolutionary dental technology. Now we are going to learn how it's possible to build wealth by coming up with a simple invention for the masses that can actually prevent accidents and loss of life.

Actor, director, and entrepreneur Anson Williams—best known for his role as Potsie on the *Happy Days* TV show in the 1970s—had a near-death experience that led him to invent a product that can save thousands of lives while still making money as a side benefit.

While exhausted and dehydrated on a long, hot summer drive through the California desert, Anson fell asleep at the wheel and nearly suffered a fatal crash. Feeling lucky to be alive, he asked his uncle—Dr. Henry Heimlich, creator of the Heimlich maneuver for saving choking victims—if there was any way to prevent drivers from falling asleep while driving.

Dr. Heimlich told Anson that biting into a lemon creates an immediate adrenaline rush that instantly makes you alert. He found this trick worked so well he developed a product, Alert Drops spray, which contains the citric acid and sour sensation of biting into a lemon.

According to a poll by the National Sleep Foundation, 168 million people reported having felt drowsy while driving. Nearly one third of drivers admitted to having fallen asleep at the wheel.

For only about ten bucks, you can buy an Alert Drops spray, keep it in your pocket or the glove compartment of your car, and spritz it on your tongue every time you feel drowsy while driving.

If you create or invest in a product that saves lives, you will make money hand over fist and feel good about it, too.

> *I find trying to solve problems and save lives more important than my film career.*
>
> —Nicole Kidman, philanthropist and
> Academy Award–winning actress

WEALTH HACK #17

Sell something right under your feet.

Flipping back a few pages to Wealth Hack #12, you'll recall that Greg Stemm goes to great lengths around the globe and across the seven seas to find and recover amazing underwater treasures. Sometimes the most lucrative marketing items are right in front of our noses—and literally right under our feet. Where some people might see a worthless pile of dirt, others see dollar signs.

When the original Yankee Stadium was torn down, a sports memorabilia dealer named Brandon Steiner bought the dirt, the bleachers, the equipment, and anything else available to create sports memorabilia his organization could sell.

The materials were repurposed and marketed to bolster a $50 million business. Fans could own an actual seat from the old stadium or a pen filled with dirt collected from the original baseball diamond. These items become everlasting keepsakes and, as with Greg Stemm's ancient coins, came with certificates of authenticity to boost the value.

The *Antiques Roadshow* in Your Own Home

If you haven't gone through your attic, now might be a good time to do so. You never know when you'll find something valuable.

A 1909 Honus Wagner baseball card in mint condition sells for millions. On an episode of the *Antiques Roadshow* television show, a man presented his great-grandfather's pocket watch. It was determined to be a 1914 Patek Philippe watch now valued at over $1.5 million. While fixing a leaky roof in the attic of their home in Toulouse, France, a family discovered a four-hundred-year-old Caravaggio painting valued in the ballpark of $136 million.

Forget the cliché: "What's in your wallet?" The real question is, "What's in your attic?"

But the real interesting stuff is in the cellar and the attic.
—Sherman Alexie, novelist, short-story
writer, poet, and filmmaker

WEALTH HACK #18

Drive the price with scarcity.

In Wealth Hack #3, Tonino Lamborghini showed us how customers will pay a fortune for a world-class product and brand name. Now we are going to add a little twist to that concept with one word: *scarcity*.

Most companies start out by originating a product, developing it, testing it, producing it, marketing it, and then distributing the daylights out of it. The goal is often to get as much shelf presence—as well as online presence—to generate consumer recognition and create a swirl of excitement and sales that will snowball into success.

But why not try the exact opposite approach?

Craig Shah, cofounder of Craig Shelly fine watches and jewelry, refuses to mass-produce his product. Instead, he creates a limited number of exclusive watches for the wealthy collector and world traveler. The watches are not only made of gold and the best quality and craftsmanship, they have a ton of fancy features such as turbo movement and twenty-two global time settings.

When entering the crowded luxury watch market, they were going right up against such established brands as Richemont, Rolex, and Louis Vuitton. The watches were over the top, but how did they break in?

Exclusive Products and Elite Services Warrant a High Price Tag

If you want to create something truly exclusive, it doesn't necessarily have to be a product that will stand the test of time (such as a watch). You could even consider extravagant *food*.

Some restaurant goers at Norma's in New York City will spend $1,000 on a lobster frittata. Serendipity 3, also located in New York, offers a frozen haute chocolate for $25,000.

People will spend ridiculous amounts on a frittata or a frozen hot chocolate in these establishments because they can't get these items anywhere else—or at least executed with the same elegance and grandeur. There is also the chance that they could be removed from the menu at any time and customers won't ever have had a chance to sample them.

Create something people will never forget, make it impossible for anyone to duplicate it, price it high, and offer it in limited supply. Those who can afford to partake in your creation will relish the moment so much, they'll be begging for seconds.

The Craig Shelly timepieces are made in such limited quantity—in the case of one product rollout, only 108—that its scarcity skyrockets the value and price. The handmade watches are numbered and sold with a certificate of authenticity. There is no online advertising; in fact, only the distributors can see the watch prior to its on-sale date. The demand multiplies until it generates a lengthy waiting list; those who don't purchase early have to wait for the next exclusive watch.

While your competitors are out trying to start a pricing war, why not be counterintuitive and go over the top with quality, design, and extra features, and charge a premium for it?

It is not with low prices, but on the contrary—it is with improved quality we cannot only hold the market, but improve it.

—Hans Wildorf, founder of Rolex

Wealth Hack #19

Offer convenience; sell convenience.

I t's not surprising to say that people today love immediate self-gratification. In our lightning-paced world, customers expect to find stuff in two clicks and have it delivered to their homes the next day. When customers have an itch to buy something, they'll scratch it right away. Online retailers like Amazon.com have raked in the dough being able to facilitate such impulse purchasing—and do it cheaply.

Whatever your business might be, think about it in two ways:

1. Does your product or service make life convenient for the customer?
2. Can you make the purchase as easy and as convenient as possible for the customer?

People flock to Trader Joe's markets not just for their uniquely curated products, but also for their speedy checkout lines and fantastic customer service. Netflix obliterated the brick-and-mortar video/DVD rental business by converting movie rentals into downloads, making purchases a click away right from the living room couch.

Think about how you are helping people save time through your product or service—as well as through the simplicity of fulfillment and receipt. If you can do both of these things— whether you are solving a problem or fulfilling a desire—you will have customers for life.

> *The average time spent in a Wawa [convenience store] is three minutes and forty-six seconds. I have a team of engineers studying how to get that down, but we still want to make it the best three minutes and forty-six seconds we can, be quick with a personal connection.*
>   —Chris Gheysens, founder of Wawa, Inc.
>   convenience store chain

PART TWO

MOGUL MINDSET

WEALTH HACK #20

*Retain your wealth by believing
that you deserve it.*

I f you do a Google search for lottery winners who lost their
fortunes or research the financial misfortunes of a great many
athletes and rock stars, you will start to notice a common theme:

*These people have attained great riches—only to lose it all
within three years.*

We all dream of that big score—our lucky break or huge
inheritance that paves the way for us to get everything we want
in life.

The challenge is, until we believe we deserve such gifts,
we will go right back to our old habits and gradually lose all of
what we have gained.

If all of the world's wealth were spread out evenly among
the population, it is estimated that most people would revert
back to their former financial status within one generation of
disbursement.

By now you have probably heard of the "law of attraction":
What we think about, we naturally draw toward us.

This is complete nonsense.

The fact is this: *We do NOT attract what we want in life, we only attract more of what we already are.*

This is why certain people who fight always seem to get into *more fights*. It's also why people who love drama attract *more drama*.

On the flip side, happy people attract *more happiness*.

Similarly, wealthy people attract *more wealth*.

How we portray ourselves—and what we think we deserve—becomes a self-fulfilling prophecy.

After all, *we are who and where we truly choose to be.*

I always knew I was going to be rich. I never doubted it for a minute.

—Warren Buffett, investor and chairman and
CEO of Berkshire Hathaway

WEALTH HACK #21

*To achieve something different, you
must DO something different.*

I n the closing chapter of *Think and Grow Rich*, "How to Out-
wit the Six Ghosts of Fear," Napoleon Hill tackled the main
issues that plague people who seek to become wealthy: indeci-
sion, doubt, and fear. One of the biggest things that hold people
back is fear of criticism and worrying about what other people
think. The most successful people simply don't care and tune
out all of that noise.

Jeff Fried, founder of All In Entertainment, was just a "regular" guy from Brooklyn, New York, who started out in aviation
and had a menial job replacing copy paper in a law firm. He
could have continued to work in either field, but instead tossed
these so-called "safe" options aside to manage a boxer.

Get this: *He knew absolutely nothing about managing a
boxer.* No one thought he could accomplish it successfully, but
that didn't stop him one bit. He shrugged off all criticism and
doubt and did something different and unexpected. In fact, the

very first fighter he signed was Riddick Bowe, who went on to become heavyweight champion of the world.

Jeff does what he likes to call *bold moves* based on his gut instinct, which he developed from the streets of Brooklyn. He has zero fear of criticism and will go all in if a deal feels right.

Don't ever be afraid to take a chance. Playing it safe will never make you a champion in your industry. Sometimes not knowing the industry you are entering and seeing it as an "outsider" can actually be to your advantage.

It's time for you to step into the ring and show off your unique moves.

Playing it safe is the riskiest choice we can make.
—Sarah Ban Breathnach, *New York Times* best-selling author

WEALTH HACK #22

Coin is king—so save your change.

So many times we find it difficult to save for that special something.

A simple trick to get started is to simply *get started*.

Take an old jar out of the cupboard and place it on the table nearest the front door. Next, place an actual image of what you desire on that jar.

Example: A trip to Hawaii with an image of palm trees and sunny beaches.

Why? The easiest way to hit a goal is to have a goal to hit. By seeing the image every day, you increase the chances of it becoming reality one hundred times over.

Now, every day you go inside, reach into your pockets or purse and dump any loose change into that jar.

Here are a few scenarios that help you contribute to the jar:

- When you check out at the grocery store and use your frequent shopper card to save seven dollars, take that newfound money you planned to spend anyway and place it into the jar the moment you walk in the door.

- When you go to lunch with friends and they offer to pick up the check that you intended to pay, place that amount into the jar the moment you walk in the door.
- When a tax refund comes through, you get a bonus from work, or even if you stumble across a few loose bills in the laundry, place all of that money into the jar the moment you walk through the door.

Small steps are more powerful than big intentions.

The progress of constant actions is the key toward any worthwhile endeavor.

Before you know it, those pennies in the jar add up to dollars, and you'll begin to see your goal materialize and be able to sink your toes in the sand.

Keep feeding your dream.

Great things are not done by impulse, but a series of small steps brought together.
           —Vincent Van Gogh, impressionist painter

Wealth Hack #23

Be kind to your future self.

One of the greatest, though unattributed, expressions in personal growth suggests that "success is achieved through *progress* and not *perfection*."

It's the incremental steps toward a worthwhile goal that give us that sense of purpose and direction.

A master was asked once by his protégée: "What can I do to ensure a life of sustained abundance?"

The answer was clear and to the point: "Be kind to your future self."

It seems we can have nearly anything we desire, as long as we are willing to pay the price.

Here's an example: We commit ourselves to being ten pounds lighter in thirty days from now. Rather than going on the latest diet fad, we can simply be kind to our "future selves" by putting down the pint of ice cream before going to bed.

Maybe the next day we'll do our future selves another favor and increase our water intake to flush our systems from the inside out.

The point is this: By taking incremental steps *today*, we are preparing ourselves for our future selves *tomorrow*.

If you're seeking wealth and prosperity for your future self, here's one thing you can do right away to lodge the concept in your mind.

Set aside ten dollars in a drawer somewhere. Don't touch it for a few weeks. When you need it—to pay for a quick lunch or a movie ticket—your future self will thank your past self that the ten bucks were waiting as a gift.

Your next steps are clear.

Do today what will be good for you down the horizon.

Sometimes it feels like a bungee cord is pulling on our butts telling us "I'm not good enough . . . I'm an impostor." Give yourself permission to love yourself.

—David M. Corbin, keynote speaker,

author, and mentor to mentors

WEALTH HACK #24

Ask yourself positive questions.

O ne of Napoleon Hill's countless messages in *Think and Grow Rich* is to learn the art of changing one's mindset from *failure consciousness* to *success consciousness*.

Instead of asking yourself self-defeating questions like "How am I going to stay in business when my top customer just went bankrupt?" you will find greater success and hidden opportunities by *rephrasing your questions as positive messages*. This will have an enormous impact on your psyche, as well as on your ability to achieve results.

Try these revisions, for example:

Instead of asking this: *Why is my business shrinking?*

Ask this: *What action steps can I take to grow my business?*

Instead of asking this: *Why am I not making enough money?*

Ask this: *How do I spend more time on the things that make me money?*

Instead of asking this: *How did I get myself into this challenge?*

Ask this: *What opportunity am I missing that I can learn from this challenge?*

Thoughts are things.

—Napoleon Hill, author *of Think and Grow Rich*

WEALTH HACK #25

Don't hold on to your nut.

Have you ever heard of the South American spider monkey? (Don't worry, there's a point to this, just hang in there . . .)

Well, spider monkeys are famous for being easy prey. All hunters need to do is spread containers around the jungle. Each container has a nut inside that lures the spider monkey. When the creature reaches its hand inside the tight opening, it inevitably clutches onto the nut.

The problem? The spider monkey's hand with the nut in it is too big to be removed through the opening. The container is way too heavy for him to lift.

The spider monkey could simply let go and get its hand out but, instead of sensing danger or giving up on the nut to do something more productive, it just sits there—right until the moment the hunter returns and makes a simple capture.

Let's leave the jungle and go back to business. Ask yourself these questions:

- *Are you holding on to beliefs about your business or industry for no reason and getting trapped?*
- *Do you rigidly stick to the same old perceptions of what works and what doesn't?*
- *Are there microtasks you are doing but shouldn't?*
- *Are you locked into incorrect negative perceptions of yourself?*

Don't be a spider monkey. Let go of your nut!

A foolish consistency is the hobgoblin of little minds.
    —Ralph Waldo Emerson, essayist and philosopher

WEALTH HACK #26

Invest twenty-six times to land one success.

M any investors and venture capitalists do all the right things, and yet they can't seem to stop failing. The failures come one after another—bang, bang, bang. It's so disheartening, especially when you read through *Forbes* and see an old friend of yours hit up with a monster success with only his second investment—one that seemed pretty dumb, yet somehow caught on.

After a dozen more disappointments—so many you want to stop counting—you are about to throw in the towel and give up. Your money is going down the drain and your confidence is funneling along with it.

The secret is this: You may only need to *get it right once.*

One success can make you millions, but the trick is that it takes *twenty-six times* to find that needle in a haystack. Among all of these, only one will balloon out and exceed expectations.

It's been shown time and time again that it takes an average of twenty-six tries before you hit your first investing home run. Don't give up after your twenty-fifth at bat.

There is a Kundalini spirit phrase that goes like this:

> *The Universe sends us exactly what we are ready for in the exact time we need it in our lives.*

Let's make a slight tweak to this to build wealth:

> *The Universe sends us exactly what we are ready* to accept.

WEALTH HACK #27

Create a vision board.

S ometimes we take for granted the most obvious things. We go about our daily work routines, pay the bills, put out fires, and shut the lights out every night, many times forgetting where we're really headed or why we're even bothering.

If asked the question "Do you have a vision for your business?" your spitfire response would probably be, "Hell, yeah—of course I do!"

But when was the last time you even looked at your vision, much less wrote it down?

Tommy Tallarico is a one-of-a-kind musician: He is probably the most successful video game music composer in the world. Not only have Tallarico's video game compositions developed a substantial following, he often performs the music live to the delight of hordes of fans.

Who ever thought video game music could be such a big deal? Tallarico did—because he had (and still has) a *vision*. He writes it down on what he calls his "vision board" and refers to it over and over again.

Tallarico likens the vision board to something of an ongoing, positive New Year's resolution. Instead of regarding this exercise as if you are failing at something and correcting it (such as losing weight), write down *exactly what you hope to accomplish in the coming year.*

The vision board should be flexible and work in the format that serves you best. You could have a giant whiteboard in your office. A screensaver or Post-it on your computer. A note or pop-up on your iPhone. Put it in any location that it works for you and serves as a constant reminder of what drives your passion and where you are headed.

Tallarico suggests forcing yourself to look at your vision board with an "outrageous" amount of regularity—as many as twenty, thirty, or forty times a day. Your goals are like mountains to climb, all of which should feed directly into your vision.

Goals = mountains.

"Nothing will stop me from getting to the top," Tallarico says. "When people climb over you or you slip, just keep on going. Climb that first mountain and you will get to the others."

Now: Go think and act like a visionary.

Dreams are extremely important. You can't do it unless you can imagine it.

　　　　—George Lucas, Hollywood producer and director

WEALTH HACK #28

Plot your next move.

The greatest entrepreneurs never remain still when it comes to looking at the future of their businesses. They are constantly plotting, planning, thinking, navigating, innovating, strategizing, and maneuvering.

Angel investor Dan Fleyshman, whom we'll revisit later in Wealth Hack #55, doesn't stop after a success. He doesn't rest on his laurels or sit back to let things simmer and play out for a while. He is constantly in search of *the next big thing*.

Dan went from being the youngest owner of a publicly traded company to founding a major poker site to investing in hoverboard products to serving as an angel investor and advisor to two dozen companies.

Hoverboards were a pretty big deal when they first came around. Suddenly we'd entered the movie *Back to the Future Part II* and could fly on skateboards like Michael J. Fox's Marty McFly.

Cool. Great. But *what's next?*

It's fine to take a breath after a success to clear your head, but after you do that, it's time to start scanning the horizon for the next opportunity. Don't pat yourself on the back and stop moving forward.

What's *your* next move? Maybe you'll become the angel investor for the first hovercar and take us from *Back to the Future* to *The Jetsons*!

You need to have a credit card to get credit.

—Dan Fleyshman, angel investor

WEALTH HACK #29

Visualize money and success.

Many of the all-time greatest athletes have used visualization techniques: Michael Jordan, Lindsey Vonn, Jack Nicklaus, Peyton Manning, and Michael Phelps, to name a few.

Did you know that celebs do the same thing? Oprah Winfrey, Will Smith, Lady Gaga, Steve Harvey, and Denzel Washington are just a few who have used visualization as a success tool.

But what about billionaires? Absolutely. Sir Richard Branson does it. Sara Blakely, self-made billionaire and Spanx founder, visualizes as well.

And so does prodigious film producer Phil Goldfine. "I *knew* I would win an Emmy. I *knew* I would win an Oscar," he says.

This isn't just boasting. It's part of Goldfine's formula for success.

Unlike the pragmatic approach of fellow entertainment Wealth Hacker Jules Haimovitz (see Wealth Hack #11), Goldfine believes in creative visualization.

No, this isn't some kind of woo-woo New Age mumbo jumbo. Creative visualization is all about the power of seeing the end goal in your mind's eye over and over again until it becomes real and then your brain subconsciously finds its way to achieve the result.

Picture the Emmy or Grammy equivalent of your industry in your mind. If money is a driving force, then visualize what a billion dollars looks like in your bank account. If you can see these things clearly, you will attain them.

Anything you can vividly imagine and ardently desire can come to pass.

—David M. Corbin, keynote speaker, author, and mentor to mentors

WEALTH HACK #30

Take action.

The author happened across a pretty smart guy in San Diego named Leo Hefner. Leo, CEO of Bluefin Management Group, posed a great question: "At all the motivational wealth-building events, how come the people in AV—such as the lighting and sound people—don't end up getting rich?"

Whoa—he had a major point! The people who work behind the scenes at events hear and see everything that goes on from all of these spectacular people. At least a few of them must be paying attention and soaking in all of the nuggets, right?

The author interviewed a few of these hardworking people and asked them point-blank: "What do you think of the speakers? Are you listening to them?" It turns out many of them *do* pay attention and like what they hear. The problem is, they admit, they never thought to *take action* about what they absorbed.

To make any wealth hack work—especially this one—you need to *think it, feel it, and get off your ass and do it.*

It's the *action* behind the law of attr*action* that makes your dreams come true.

> *Vision without action is merely a dream. Action without*
> *vision just passes the time. Vision with action can*
> *change the world.*
>
> —Joel A. Barker, business futurist

WEALTH HACK #31

Accept what is given to you.

The most successful people in the world know how to accept what is given to them: help, resources, ideas, and connections. The people who think they can do everything on their own may be smart and industrious, but they don't accrue *abundance*.

There is no benefit to trying to go the distance alone and no shame in asking for assistance from experts. Pride can be the one thing holding you back.

Challenge yourself! For thirty days, accept all that is offered to you. Even if you are invited to a party but have other plans, say, "I would love to but I can't make it this time. But keep me on the list for next time . . . or how about we make plans for coffee and catch up in person?"

When we accept what is gifted to us, we offer the giver a chance to feel appreciated. Let's say someone offers you a container of homemade chocolate cookies, and you decline because you're on a diet. How do you know that person didn't stay up for hours baking them just for you—only to feel rejected by you?

Accept the gift. Thank the individual for being so generous.

You don't have to ruin your diet by eating the container of cookies. Bring them home for your family to enjoy. Or place them in the office pantry and let your coworkers have at them. Without a doubt, they will be devoured and turned into a pile of crumbs within minutes.

> *As we express our gratitude, we must never forget that the highest appreciation is not to utter words, but to live by them.*
>
> —John F. Kennedy, thirty-fifth president of the United States

WEALTH HACK #32

Treat your life as if it were your cell phone.

M ost people worship their cell phones. Some people treat them with even greater care and TLC than they do their own loved ones. They know where their phones are at all times, make sure they are properly charged, and perform a big chunk of their daily functions on them. Some people are hopelessly addicted and can't turn away from their smartphones for a second in case they might buzz, ring, or notify them about a trending social media post.

Imagine this: *What if we ran our lives the way we do our cell phones?*

Our cell phones are a direct reflection on how we conduct our lives. If our apps are out of date, if we have a hundred unread emails or cracked screens, we feel overwhelmed, disjointed, and crappy. If we lose our chargers and our phones are depleted at only 2 percent power, we feel weak and powerless.

On the flip side, when we receive and charge up the latest iPhone or Android and successfully transfer our lives onto it, we feel energized, connected, scheduled, updated, dialed in, and organized. We feel like we can take on the world.

Adopt the mindset that your life is always a brand-new, fully charged, and loaded mobile phone in mint condition. If you do, your life will always have a clear signal and you will rule your universe.

> *When you treat yourself right, you run better and more efficiently. Which means you don't have to go one hundred miles an hour to get everything done.*
>
> —Ann Curry, journalist and photojournalist

WEALTH HACK #33

Explain your why—*not just
your* who *and* what.

When meeting with prospective new clients and partners, most people have a tendency to jump into telling *who* they are and *what* they do.

Here's how it goes: "Hi, my name is Cy, the real estate guy."

That is perfectly normal and fine—Cy is the *who* and real estate is the *what*—but it's also pretty *blah* (even though it does rhyme). It doesn't exactly *wow* the other parties or make Cy memorable.

In order to make yourself truly stand out, you need to provide the *who*, the *what*, and the **why**. Instead of just "I'm Cy, the real estate guy," why not add some detail and explanation to it? Provide *why* you went into real estate in the first place, as it is so much more impactful.

Cy might say something like, "I'm Cy, the real estate guy. When I was young, I watched as my Uncle Jimmy's home was foreclosed on, and he had to rent a dingy apartment in a bad neighborhood. It devastated him. To this day, that disappointment sticks with him. It was at that moment I decided to make a career out of helping home buyers."

The *why* has provided an emotional context for the potential customers and partners about Cy. Others will regard him as an emotionally caring person who lives and breathes his family and business. He has become memorable and someone with whom people want to do business.

Tell me the facts and I'll learn. Tell me the truth and I'll believe. But tell me a story and it will live in my heart forever.

—Native American proverb

WEALTH HACK #34

Reverse mental conditioning.

To varying degrees, we are the products of our backgrounds and experiences. If we went through hardships and traumas during our childhoods, those situations and events can linger with us throughout our lives—even if we spend years on a therapist's couch.

Consciously or unconsciously holding on to these mental images and feelings can hold us back from achieving abundance. Legendary motivational guru Les Brown has plowed through tons of success books and found that not a single one addresses the issue of how to *reverse* this mental conditioning that haunts us and prevents us from reaching our goals and becoming wealthy.

Les knows all about letting go of mental baggage. When he was growing up dirt poor in Miami, Florida, his school described him as "mentally retarded." He spent many years overcoming this false label, building confidence, and releasing the mental conditioning that caused so much pain. Once freed from the past, he was able to rise up to become a member of the Ohio

House of Representatives, a powerful motivational speaker, a published author, and a successful radio/TV host.

They Became Self-Made Mega-Successes—So Can You

It *is* possible to become a self-made billionaire.

All of these individuals went from rags to riches:

- Oprah Winfrey: She went from a poverty-stricken childhood to TV talk show host to queen of a mega-business empire valued at nearly $3 billion.
- Howard Schultz: He was raised in federally subsidized housing in Brooklyn, New York, became CEO of Starbucks, and has a net worth of $3 billion.
- Ralph Lauren: Born Ralph Lipschitz, the son of poor Jewish immigrants, he went on to become one of the world's wealthiest, most iconic fashion designers with $7 billion in net worth.
- George Soros: After witnessing the Nazi occupation of Hungary and then fleeing the Communist Hungarian regime, he has since amassed an $8.3 billion fortune from his investments.
- Larry Ellison: He grew up on the tough South Side of Chicago with a father who told him he was "good for nothing," and he has now made $57.6 billion as an entrepreneur and cofounder of Oracle Corporation.

If these individuals could overcome their challenges and rise to the top, so can you!

What is holding you back? Release it *starting today.*

We might be through with the past, but the past is not through with us.

　　　　　　　　　—Les Brown, legendary motivational speaker

WEALTH HACK #35

Reward yourself with achievement.

We all deserve a reward every now and then. A trip to our favorite clothier, shoe store, jeweler, or sports car dealer can be gratifying.

After you have succeeded at something—a lucrative business deal, a profitable marketing campaign, a touted speaking engagement, etc.—by all means reward yourself. However, the next time you do it, instead of heading to your favorite store or boutique, *invest in something that gives back to you.*

Have you considered buying a software program on learning a new language? Taking an online course? Learning a craft? Reading a book?

Make personal growth and learning something new a line-item expense. You never know when your newfound skill will lead to financial gain.

Formal education will make you a living; self-education will make you a fortune.
—Jim Rohn, entrepreneur, author, and motivational speaker

PART THREE

MAKING IT
HAPPEN

WEALTH HACK #36

Stick to your core; outsource the rest.

Retired construction and engineering executive Ron Graham has powerful advice for any entrepreneurial organization looking to crack the wealth code without cracking itself in the process.

Outsource.

That may be a bad word to some people and companies. Sometimes it's really hard to let go. Don't you want ownership and control of every deal? And why share your hard-earned take with another company?

So many companies fail because they try to do things that fall outside their areas of expertise. Or, they take on projects that tax their resources and distract them from the real money-making deals. Or, they agree to do the work even though it's going to cost a fortune to execute and will hit into profits.

What did Graham do when he needed to excavate a building site that was too costly? "We outsourced it to another company—a subcontractor," he answered. "The subcontractor could do it more cheaply."

It doesn't matter if a subcontractor makes a buck from your deal. The subcontractor knows how to manage the costs on that particular aspect of the project, and so it becomes their problem—not yours. At the end of the day, it frees up your company to make *more deals* and take on projects that are in your power alley and more profitable in the long run.

By sticking to its core—pouring concrete—Graham Group Ltd. went from a $3 million company to a $2 billion company. That's a hefty slab of dough!

Master your strengths, outsource your weaknesses.
—Ryan Kahn, career coach

WEALTH HACK #37

Tap into the power of a fulcrum.

Yes, we know it's a funky word: *fulcrum*.

A fulcrum is the little ball or leverage point on a seesaw. The more we move that point toward one direction, the greater torque and power we have.

The wealthy understand that leverage is the single most important principle for personal achievement.

In the early days of the tech industry, companies such as Apple and Microsoft made money coming and going. They controlled the fulcrum and therefore controlled everything.

Think about the iPhone, for example. Apple didn't just create a phone. They created a universe of accessories for hungry consumers: earbuds, carrying cases, cables, wall chargers, and screen protectors.

Other companies also tapped into the iPhone fulcrum, competing on these companion products by creating "designer" screen protectors, skins, selfie sticks, and other enhancements.

Either way, Apple is happy to allow room for the tagalongs when it's their product directly at the center of the consumer frenzy.

If you see a modern gold rush happening, don't just follow the herd and dig for gold. Search for the fulcrum.

Give me a lever long enough and a fulcrum on which to place it, and I shall move the world.
—Archimedes, ancient Greek mathematician

WEALTH HACK #38

Save 50 percent; spend 50 percent.

When starting a business, *do not overleverage*. Period.
Call it what you like: bootstrapping your business, tightening your belt, cutting corners.

It's all right to borrow a bit here and there, but you never want to owe so much you might be drowning in debt if the worst-case scenario were to arise. Sometimes things occur that are beyond your control—such as an economic downturn—but you can safeguard against that as well.

Whereas many of his contemporaries came and went over the years, wealthy South California land and real estate investor Marshall Ezralow survived and thrived through *four recessions*.

While competitors built to cut back, Ezralow managed to create all-inclusive apartments and beat competitors on both price and value. His apartments featured all the extras—pool, Jacuzzi, furniture—and yet he found ways to avoid taking on too much debt. It's less money in the short term, but a lot more in the long term.

Ezralow's advice is to have about 50 percent of the company in equity and 50 percent leveraged—not a penny more!

Beware of little expenses. A small leak will sink a great ship.

> —Benjamin Franklin, scientist, inventor, author, and statesman

WEALTH HACK #39

Invest like a farmer.

How do the world's most successful investors always seem to know the right time to buy, sell, or hold?

Nik Halik—an entrepreneurial alchemist, investor, and 5 Day Weekend strategist who has explored the *Titanic* underwater, as well the Earth from the edge of space—believes the secret to smart investing, property entry/exit, and business acquisition/exit is *thinking like a farmer*. "They know when to plant and when to harvest. It's the same concept."

For Halik, there are patterns, or "economic seasons," when stocks are low, high, and stagnant. The people who know when to place their bets, unload, or stick are the ones who win out every time.

All investing seasons are *driven by human emotions*. Most people invest with their hearts on their sleeves and are guided by two main drivers: *fear of losing money* and *the greed of making money*. (The former is much stronger than the latter.) These emotional drivers create the economic investing seasons.

Halik has used this investing methodology with tremendous success for more than two decades. By comparing the economic cycles (years) to the four seasons—summer, fall, winter, and spring—he can superimpose them onto what he refers to as an "economic seasonal clock" (see image below).

The clock begins at 12:00, which is the *economic summer*. As a farmer, this is when you would begin to store the hay in the shed to prepare for fall. Similarly, as an investor, you need to tighten your belt, cut back on spending, and stockpile funds.

Fall starts at 3:00: share prices, commodity prices, and overseas reserves all begin to decline. Money becomes scarce as monetary policy is tightened. Between the fall (3:00) and winter (6:00), you may start to buy out your competitors who are tensing up from the looming economic dark clouds.

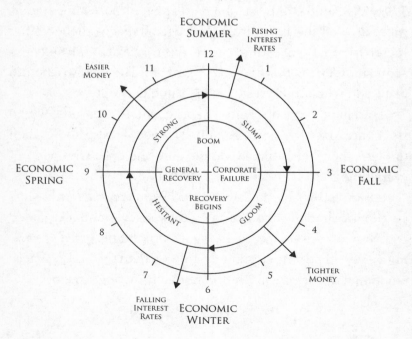

By 6:00, winter has begun; the economy is in recession. (We witnessed this in 2008 with foreclosures, bankruptcies, and bailouts.) Instead of running in fear for shelter with the rest of the herd, what does the savvy farmer do? He goes the opposite route and uses his summer stockpile to buy up some great bargains. For company owners, this means purchasing businesses that don't have enough reserves to survive the winter. For property and land owners, this means buying up everything possible (i.e., foreclosures) at the lowest prices.

At 9:00, we enter spring: The economy gradually returns to normal. Investors start to feel more comfortable and are looking for things to buy. This is when you sell off investments as they rise toward their peak values.

The complete economic cycle—summer to summer or 12:00 to 12:00—lasts about eight to eleven years. Summer (12:00, the top of an economic boom) through winter (6:00, the bust) is about three to four years.

The main Wealth Hack to be gleaned is this: Be aware that all investment decisions, and thus economic factors, are driven by human emotions. The best time to buy is when everyone is most afraid during the economic winter, and everything is spiraling downward. The prime time to sell is when prices are at their peak and people are at their greediest.

> *You're not working for money. You're working for
> freedom. You're working for a 5 Day Weekend lifestyle.*
> > —Nik Halik, entrepreneurial alchemist,
> > investor, and 5 Day Weekend strategist

WEALTH HACK #40

Know every aspect of your deal.

I t may be difficult to believe, but many businesspeople don't close as many deals as they like because they fail to do enough research.

Knowledge isn't just power. You must have the kind of knowledge that is elusive to the average person and yet is valued by the customer.

In the real estate business, for example, real estate agent and host of *Million Dollar Listing Los Angeles* Josh Flagg believes that knowledge is what separates 1 percent of successful realtors from the other 99 percent. It's why some real estate agents make the big deals in the tens of millions versus those who are relegated to the six-figure society.

As a kid, Flagg studied every single house in the Beverly Hills area. He learned early on that if he sold more expensive luxury homes starting at $4 million, he didn't have to work nearly as many hours as the agents selling houses for $400K.

When doing a deal—whether in real estate or something else—always dive deep into the details. If you know the details and you know its value, that's when you'll know your own as well. Never settle for less than what you're worth.

Josh Flagg has never lowered his commission, and neither should you.

> *Real estate investing, even on a very small scale, remains a tried and true means of building an individual's cash flow and wealth.*
>
> —Robert Kiyosaki, founder of the Rich Dad Company and author of *Rich Dad Poor Dad*

WEALTH HACK #41

Go against the grain—
work with your competitors.

C ompetition is the new collaboration. Why are there four
gas stations on every main intersection? Would you rather
start your restaurant on a dirt road or situate it alongside restaurant row in the best part of town?

Some may see this type of competition as a bad thing, but
businesses can often help each other. When things go terribly
awry in your industry, for example, many companies have the
attitude that *everyone must fend for themselves.* What do you
suppose happens in those circumstances? It's not one ship that
goes down, but the entire fleet.

Ernesto Ancira, Jr., who owns a slew of auto dealerships
throughout the San Antonio, Texas, area, doesn't think this way
at all. This has been to the benefit of the industry, the community, and even his own business, Ancira-Winton Chevrolet, Inc.

When the economy went down, Ernesto joined with his
competitors and the Texas Automobile Dealers Association to
reverse the negative image of the auto industry in their area.

They worked as a team and everyone benefitted—primarily because they created a level of sustained trust between consumer and dealer.

What can you do to partner with your competitors and help raise the image of your industry?

> *The problem with competition is that it takes away the requirement to set your own path, to invent your own method, to find a new way.*
> —Seth Godin, entrepreneur, blogger, and marketer

WEALTH HACK #42

Convert customers with words.

The world of copywriting is all about one thing: *conversion.* In any kind of advertising—online, print, television, or radio—you have to be able to connect with masses of customers in such a way that they are willing to plunk down hard-earned cash for your product and send revenue your way that far exceeds the cost of the ad.

In short, copywriters write words that lure people in to buy products.

Easier said than done, right?

World-class direct-response copywriter Craig Clemens has the gift of being able to create this type of mass conversion from just a single ad. Clemens, the cofounder of Golden Hippo Media, has turned $1 billion in sales—now *that's* conversion!

The mistake he's seen time and time again in failed copy is that it lacks insights directly from the customer. So often entrepreneurs and business professionals channel what *they* think when trying to market their products or services. Who cares what *they* think?

For example, suppose you've created a supplement you believe is fantastic and can help people with a wide range of mind/body/spirit issues. How do you come up with the magic words in an ad that will convert mass sales?

You ask a perspective customer point-blank: "What really bothers you?"

The answer comes in: "I don't know. I just feel all stressed out . . . being stressed out all the time makes me unhappy and then I can't think straight and then I can't get things done."

Bam! You have your answer. The copy must tell a story about a woman who is stressed out at work, at home, and so on and lost her ability to focus and get things accomplished. Then she found your supplement. After just a couple of days, she started to feel happier and less stressed out. Plus, she's gotten a lot more done.

In the above scenario, you've been able to convey a relatable story because you have gotten into the customer's shoes and can understand her struggles. The customer follows along with the story, sees how it plays out, and wants the same positive result as the person in the ad from taking the supplement. This way she can visualize herself in the story and want the product for herself. *Voila!* Conversion.

It takes a big idea to attract the attention of consumers and get them to buy your product. Unless your advertising contains a big idea, it will pass like a ship in the night. I doubt if more than one campaign in a hundred contains a big idea.

—David Ogilvy, founder of Ogilvy & Mather
advertising firm

WEALTH HACK #43

Hire a brain.

There's an old saying: "Work your strengths, hire your weaknesses." In Wealth Hack #36, Ron Graham recommended that you "stick to your core and outsource the rest."

Here's an even more explicit variation of these ideas. Walter O'Brien, the real-life genius behind the TV show *Scorpion*, advises: "Every day you should hire a 'rent a brain.'"

What he means is that you should have access to the smartest, best people with expertise in areas that fall outside your power alley.

By hiring a "rent a brain," you can focus on your vision and goals and let the geniuses take care of the details. If you have a strong business idea but are terrible with numbers, hire the smartest CFO. If you have brilliant marketing ideas but aren't a strong writer, hire the most talented copywriter. If you want to invent a product but don't have the technical know-how, hire a brilliant scientist.

Don't be afraid to recruit experts and people smarter than you in specific areas. You'll free up your time and save yourself a lot of anguish and headaches.

Surround yourself with people you have respect for, not the people you have influence over.

—Anonymous

WEALTH HACK #44

Create a land of misfit toys.

It's become a cliché that every business owner seeks to hire, train, and retain the best people possible and create an "all-star" team. But does hiring "the best" always mean the team will gel and produce something spectacular? Not necessarily.

You don't need to be a baseball fan to understand this metaphor. The 2011 Boston Red Sox were a *stacked* team and a clear-cut favorite to head to the World Series. They were compared with the greatest teams of all time, including the 1927 New York Yankees. On top of proven superstars such as David Ortiz, Jacoby Ellsbury, and Dustin Pedroia, they added a solid hitter in Carl Crawford and slugger first baseman Adrián González. How could they lose? And yet, the team was an utter mess of dysfunction with players not getting along, failing to play up to expectations, and some infamously drinking beer and eating fried chicken in the clubhouse. The team finished a disappointing third in the division, and manager Terry Francona and general manager Theo Epstein abandoned ship during the

off-season. The team ended up trading away newcomers Crawford and González.

In business, why do some unbelievable teams fail like the
2011 Red Sox? People say it's the right chemistry combined
with just the right mix of talent that wins—not necessarily the
best talent in every single position.

But what does the "right chemistry" really mean? People
who compliment and hug each other all day?

Stephen Van Deventer, chairman and chief executive officer
at Preveceutical Medical Inc., throws out the unique idea that
to form a chemical bond, every member of the team must:

1. **Be positive at all times:** Winning teams all consist of
   members who have skin in the game and a deep faith
   that the plan will work. Positivity becomes contagious.
   Similarly, even the slightest negativity can spread through
   a company like a contagion. All negative thinkers should
   hop right off the bus.
2. **Represent strength in different sectors:** Why employ
   people who know all the same stuff? That would produce
   pretty lame results.
3. **Have connections:** These are folks who know people
   in a range of areas. Sure, it's fun if the team members
   are friends and buddies and travel in the same circles.
   But that won't enrich the pool of company contacts
   and breadth of outside expertise that may need to be
   called upon.

When all assembled, the above elements tend to draw in
motivated and quirky people who are driven by the energy and

enthusiasm of others. They succeed in certain environments where they are granted ample creative space in which to explore and soar with others who are as committed to the cause as they are.

Van Deventer likens this to "creating the land of the misfit toys." While working at other companies, they probably failed in some way and were forced into rigid compartments. They became disenchanted and "broken" until, at last, they finally found themselves among a group of *other misfit toys*.

Think of pretty much any extraordinary team depicted in movies; they're almost always misfits who complement each other's strengths and weaknesses in major ways.

Check out these films and you'll immediately get the point: all of the *Star Trek*, *Star Wars*, *Avengers*, and *Toy Story* flicks (okay, this last one is obvious); *Ocean's Eleven*; *The Dirty Dozen*; *The Untouchables*; and *The Magnificent Seven*.

> *If you're trying to create a company, it's like baking a cake. You have to have all the ingredients in the right proportion.*
>
> —Elon Musk, founder of Tesla, Inc. and
> SpaceX and cofounder of PayPal

WEALTH HACK #45

Own your community.

It's not enough to have a ton of friends, followers, and fans. You have to constantly build your community, serve it, and engage it.

As of this writing, TV and podcast host Jeffrey Hayzlett has over a gazillion followers. He started out building his community one at a time by cultivating his niche in a specific area—the C-Suite network—and then *owning* that space. If you Google "C-Suite" and "celebrity" one name pops up first: Jeffrey Hayzlett.

By owning the community in your area and proving to followers you are the bona fide expert, you develop a powerhouse base and achieve unlimited things in entertainment, politics, and any other category. You can move entire markets.

From having set himself up as an all-time great, Hayzlett has become the single biggest go-to person for anyone who is seeking business and corporate advice.

Where can you position yourself as the all-time authority in your chosen field of endeavor?

One Million: The Magic Number

Social media moguls have a secret: They know the floodgates open once you reach *one million* "likes" and/ or "followers" on platforms such as Twitter, Instagram, Snapchat, Facebook, and the next one on the horizon.

One million is the magic number. Not only is that a ton of people, but with a million eyeballs, you become what is known as a "super influencer" a la Kim Kardashian—a power broker who doesn't have to do much of anything to build exponential wealth.

By getting one million followers, you are gaining customers for life who will buy stuff from you without your having to do a thing.

How does one amass such a large following? Well, that could be another whole book. In addition to Jeffrey Hayzlett's advice, the main thing is to be *authentic—*meaning, *be yourself.* Don't pretend to be something you are not, or fake being an authority, as readers will see right through it.

The key is to connect with and engage your community. Offer your followers things no one else can—and pay constant attention to them. It's all about FOP: Frequency of Post.

MORE ENGAGEMENT = MORE EYE-
BALLS = HIGHER RATE OF RETURN.

If you want to grow a social presence, you have to take the time and energy to attract the low-hanging fruit: your current customers and other people who know you. From there, you'll gain other fans and followers who are likely to eventually buy from you. But you have to start with your current customers.

—Dave Kerpen, entrepreneur and
cofounder of Likeable Media

WEALTH HACK #46

Use the ARCS method to grab customers.

In Wealth Hack #42, you learned from a pro—copywriter extraordinaire Craig Clemens—how to lure in customers. Now you are ready for his advanced class on ARCS:

A = ASK A QUESTION.
R = REVEAL YOU'VE BEEN THERE.
C = CALL OUT YOUR DISCOVERY.
S = SEND THEM OUT TO DO SOMETHING.

Clemens illustrates this method with an example from caveman days.

A = Ask a question **that introduces the problem.**
Marty's brother was eaten by a bear. How do you kill a bear?

R = Reveal you've been there, **which shows you can relate to the problem.**
Say, my brother was wounded by a bear, too . . .

C = Call out your discovery **to show you experienced the problem but you found a way to solve it.**
I managed to kill the bear and save my brother in the nick of time—just by stabbing him with this amazing spear I created. My friend Bill used it, too, and it worked to kill a wolf . . . You'll take one for your next hunt? Great! That will cost you twenty apples.

S = Send them out to do something **and stay engaged.**
When you come back from hunting, let me know how it worked. I'd love to hear your feedback.

With the ARCS method, you aren't just creating customers— you are also building relationships of confidence and trust that will be remembered every time they use the spear. They'll be even more receptive when you pitch them your next product, the slingshot.

> *People want to be told what to do so badly they'll listen to anyone.*
> —Don Draper (character on AMC's TV show *Mad Men*)

WEALTH HACK #47

*Hire people with high EQ to babysit
the people with high IQ.*

I t would be really simple for a start-up company to have one
single hiring criteria: Only recruit the people who have the
highest IQ.

This sort of makes sense, right? You want to bring in people
who are highly intelligent, think on their feet, work independ-
ently, stay focused, and problem solve.

Well, IQ is only one factor in hiring and certainly not the
be-all and end-all. Creativity is a factor, depending on the type
of business; in all likelihood, you need people who can create
a new box, not just measure its size. As Stephen Van Deventer
explored in Wealth Hack #44, the best teams may be likened
to "a land of misfit toys."

Walter O'Brien, the brains behind the *Scorpion* TV show
and true-to-life über problem solver, believes there is yet another
key ingredient in creating a team: EQ (emotional quotient),
which measures emotional intelligence. In many cases, though
certainly not all, people with high IQs tend to have low EQs.

Why? Chances are, they were bullied in school because of their brains (and lack of coolness) and therefore have learned to shut down their emotions as a defense mechanism.

By hiring enough people with off-the-charts EQ, you are ensuring that you have a balanced, even-keeled team that can communicate and cooperate. In all likelihood, the high IQ folks will help the high EQ people with their technical problems; at the same time, the high EQ people will babysit the high IQ folks and ensure that everyone plays along nicely in the sandbox. Your company parties will also be a lot more fun.

> *In a high-IQ job pool, soft skills like discipline, drive,*
> *and empathy mark those who emerge as outstanding.*
> —Daniel Goleman, psychologist, science journalist,
> author of *Emotional Intelligence*

Wealth Hack #48

Leverage MIC.

A MIC is not just what you drop when you've said or done something triumphant to a person or group of people. It's also an acronym that stands for the following:

M = Methodical
I = Information
C = Code

Very successful people leverage MIC all the time. It's a tool they use to capitalize on the good and bad of the people around them and in their workplace.

If, for example, you have someone working in sales who isn't giving you the results you wanted and isn't incentivized by salary increases and extra bonus rewards, you can dig for information about this person to help get the needed result. Perhaps you discover that this same salesperson has a child who wants a toy that is hard to get. What do you do with this information? You could track down and purchase the toy for the salesperson to give to the child. In doing so, you'll hit a soft spot and be able to use it as leverage so you can both get what you want.

In business, you could set a new quota for that person to reach and, in doing so, sales go up and their personal commissions rise. At the same time, the kid gets an awesome surprise upon arriving home. In other words, everybody wins.

This scenario is effective because you've hit the individual's hot button (aka Code) to gain more leverage and inspire the employee to perform better without any kind of criticism, negativity, or threat whatsoever.

Some of this may sound a bit manipulative—and, to some degree, it is. Wealthy people have found it to be far more effective than harsher alternatives and use it all the time. The entire purpose of MIC is that you are gathering the information methodically, in sequence, and then acting on that information in a way that is positive and uplifting.

To get what you want, help others get what they want first.
—Zig Ziglar, salesman and motivational speaker

Wealth Hack #49

Hire the best—and cry only once.

Many business owners cheapen out when it comes to recruiting. They hire the first living, breathing person with a pulse they believe will get the job done and put an end to the miserable, unending recruiting process. They believe they're saving money by not hiring high-end top performers.

Wrong.

The key is to *spend the most to get the best*. Sure, it's painful to have to weed through dozens of candidates and spend months conducting a job search. It may also cost a bundle to bring in an executive recruiting firm to find that exact right fit for your company. But it's worth every second of time spent and every penny invested.

If you settle on a mediocre employee, that person may turn out "okay" and get the job done. But if you want to break revenue records, how could "mediocre" possibly be the answer?

For critical roles in marketing, sales, finance, and operations, you always want to hire the top people. Ask yourself these questions about the candidate:

1. Does she have the potential to challenge my team and me to work harder and do better?
2. Does she have skills, talent, and experience I don't?
3. Does she have a proven track record generating revenue?
4. Does she have knowledge from other winning companies?
5. Does she have fire in the belly to drive a business?

If the answer is "yes" to all of the above, open your wallet and keep your ego in check. Many business owners feel threatened by bringing in someone who may be smarter, more talented, or more experienced than they are regarding their products, services, or industry. That is absurd. You *want* to improve your team by filling in gaps in talent and experience that you don't have—why else bother hiring someone?

Here's an obvious example. If you are a teenage John Lennon forming a band, you want to bring in a gifted musician like Paul McCartney, even though he may be your equal in talent and sometimes challenge your thinking and dominance. (Of course, McCartney was not Lennon's employee in any fashion, and they later became equal musical partners—but you get the idea.)

Hiring the best will likely cost you a bundle in salaries, hiring bonuses, and recruiting fees. You'll feel a little pain and shed some tears upfront and risk having to occasionally defer to someone else's superior knowledge, but, in the long run, you will reap the rewards and profits of the gifts these individuals bring to your company.

If each of us hires people who are smaller than we are, we shall become a company of dwarfs. But if each of us hires people who are bigger than we are, we shall become a company of giants.

—David Ogilvy, founder of Ogilvy & Mather advertising firm

WEALTH HACK #50

Speak at an Ivy League university.

If you want to supplement your career and substantially widen your business and your brand by becoming a public speaker, there is one thing you can do that immediately builds gravitas: Speak at Harvard, Yale, or Princeton. If you do this, you'll open up doors and quadruple your business.

The main way to land a speaking gig at an Ivy League university is to network through the alumni associations. Get to know as many alumni as possible on a professional level to stir up some buzz about you and then move on to outreaching the people who run the alumni associations.

The staffs at alumni organizations are always on the hunt for superb speakers with engaging, relevant topics. But don't "pitch" yourself right away or you risk scaring them off with too hard of a sell. First make introductions and then later share sample clips of your finest, most professional speaking engagements that conclude with thunderous applause and ovations. Once you have them hooked, suggest a few topics and be sure to send them rave reviews from your previous engagements.

Once you are able to get a speaking engagement at one of these institutions, you are as good as gold. That credential can appear on your website, in your professional biography, and on your social media pages. It becomes part of how you are introduced at your other speaking engagements and is a calling card for life.

An Ivy League speaking engagement will open doors for you and ensure that you will be remembered. People will pay attention to you when you speak and will always regard you as the smartest, most qualified person in the room.

Tradition is a very powerful force.
—John Kotter, Konosuke Matsushita Professor of Leadership, Emeritus at the Harvard Business School, and founder of Kotter International

WEALTH HACK #51

Amplify the customer's request.

I magine creating a business in which you could help people meet their celebrity idols, break into exclusive establishments, and fulfill their wildest dreams.

Steve Sims, the owner of a company called Bluefish, does all that—and more. He's a real-life Wizard of Oz. He helped one client get serenaded by Elton John. He facilitated a couple getting married by the pope. He even sent a group of people in a submarine down to the bow of the *Titanic*.

You may not have Sims's *chutzpah* and contacts to do exactly what he does, but he recommends one thing you *should do* with all of your customers: *amplify the request.*

What does this mean? Simply: Kick it up a notch. Go the extra step for your customers.

Here are some examples:

- In addition to arranging for Elton John perform for the customer, the musician also gave the client a piano lesson.

- In addition to introducing the customer to the rock band Journey and watching them perform, he staged the event so that the customer performed on stage with them.
- In addition to setting up a private dinner party for six at the feet of Michelangelo's *David* in Florence, he brought in Italian singer Andrea Bocelli as the evening's entertainment.

Ask yourself: What unexpected thing can you do for your customers that totally *wows* them?

There are no traffic jams along the extra mile.
     —Roger Staubach, NFL Hall of Fame quarterback

WEALTH HACK #52

*Get celebrities to be photographed
with your product.*

I f your company created a product that isn't getting the attention it deserves, there is one thing you can do to give it a
major boost and raise its profile: Photograph a celebrity using
it, wearing it, or just holding it. That picture will garner a lot
of attention for the product, your brand, and your company,
building instant recognition.

Gavin Keilly, CEO of GBK Productions, is known as one
of the top "gift lounge connoisseurs." In other words, he's the
person who coordinates the swag—the free stuff for attendees at
high-class parties, fund-raisers, and other events. If your product is selected in the mix of offerings, there is a good chance a
well-known celebrity will be photographed with it. You can then
plaster that picture all over social media without it being considered advertising—and people will respond with excitement.
It benefits your company's image even more if the photograph
takes place at a charitable event.

Attract Star Power

Celebrity endorsements can do amazing things to raise exposure for your product or service. In fact, big-name endorsements are the number-one driving force behind millennials' online purchasing.

The major caution: These "name brands" can plummet if scandals surface. Famous athletes, actors, and musicians have all been known to lose major ad campaigns due to various degrees of misconduct. This is just a short list of celebs who were dropped from major campaigns due to scandals: Tiger Woods, Matt Lauer, O.J. Simpson, Bill Cosby, Lance Armstrong, and Gilbert Gottfried.

Choose your celebs wisely.

In one instance, Keilly had a client who offered his company's watch to all guests as part of the swag bag. Rock star Ozzy Osbourne grabbed the watch and placed it in his mouth. The photograph was worth a mint for the client's brand.

What product do you have that can go in Ozzy's mouth? Never mind—don't answer that. All you need to do is look for the right match of event and celebrity with your product or service.

A picture is worth a thousand words.

—Anonymous

WEALTH HACK #53

Invest in precious metals.

A century ago, one ounce of gold worth about twenty dollars could buy a magnificent men's suit. Today, it's impossible to buy *any* suit for twenty dollars.

And yet, that same amount of gold—*one ounce*—is currently worth well over a thousand dollars. That's plenty of money to buy a high-end designer suit.

The value of gold goes up and down, but over the long haul it's a safe bet because it weathers most storms and keeps up with inflation. Gold obviously doesn't collect interest or dividends, but the value tends to go up when other areas decline so it's good to have some gold coins safely stashed away in addition to your other investments.

Diamonds—and Other Precious Metals—Are Forever

Plenty of billionaires have made their fortunes in precious metals and still do. These are just a few billionaires who continue to view gold as a viable investing area: Ray Dalio, David Einhorn, Stanley Druckenmiller, and Lord Jacob Rothschild.

South African billionaire Christo Wiese started out by creating a chain of Shoprite supermarkets in Cape Town, but over the years he has been actively investing in diamond mines. In Australia, Gina Rinehart became the world's sixth-wealthiest female billionaire by overseeing companies that dig for iron ore and coal.

You don't need to be Gollum from *Lord of the Rings* to seek out the "precious." Consult with your financial advisor and ask about gold ETFs (exchange-traded funds) and other investing methods to determine if precious metals are a good place for you to start.

Gold is money. Everything else is credit.
—J. P. Morgan, financier and banker

PART FOUR

WINNING
WISDOM

WEALTH HACK #54

*Buy a gumball machine and make
your money stick to more money.*

I f you were to ask the wealthiest people in the world the question "What is the one thing you all have in common?" what do you think they would say?

"Residual income," they'd all answer.

What on earth is that?

Residual income is doing something once and getting paid for it over and over again.

Here's how it works to generate a life of sustained abundance.

Let's say one hundred people are given $1,000 cash. Each one of them wants a brand-new sofa for the living room. What do you suppose 90 percent of them would do?

Buy a sofa, right? Then they would spend $1,500 for that sofa and go in debt for $500.

The top 9 percent would buy a sofa for $1,000 or less and live debt free. How many of those people do we know?

However, the millionaires and billionaires would do something completely different from that 99 percent.

They would go out and buy an inexpensive bubble gum machine. You know, those bright-red tall ones you see in the mall. They contain colored gumballs that spin down a chute while the kids eagerly await their prize. These machines cost around $750.

The millionaires and billionaires take the remaining $250 and buy bubble gum balls in bulk for a few cents each. They place the gumball machine at a local store where kids come by and plunk quarters into the slots to receive their treats.

Basically, the wealthy are trading in a quarter for pennies over and over. In no time, they are making $1,000 in profit. They use that revenue to buy the sofa and live debt free.

The wealthiest people understand the importance of creating a machine that will continue to make them money month after month after month without spending an additional dime.

This concept can translate to a host of other ideas. An author could write a best-selling book and receive royalties forever. Another person may invent a product that receives dividends for generations.

The key is to create your own version of that machine and have it make money for decades. All you need to do is set it on autopilot and refill the gumballs.

That is the magic of residual income.

The key to wealth is to do something once and get paid for it over and over again.

—Anonymous

WEALTH HACK #55

Don't be afraid to give to get.

When angel investor Dan Fleyshman was trying to get placement for his power-drink idea, Who's Your Daddy, he needed to find a way to place his product on the shelves.

Dan gave the drink to 7-Eleven on a trial basis *for free*. He believed in the product so much that he was willing to take his chances, just to get shelf exposure. After the drink proved itself with customer sales, 7-Eleven stocked it (and paid for it).

Once consumer interest was established, Dan went to Albertson's, Costco, and other retailers and told the 7-Eleven success story (but, of course, leaving out the part about the free-trial basis).

Here's another example of the same principle from a different Wealth Hacker. In the late 1970s, innovator Ron Klein noticed that when Wall Street bond traders needed bond quotes while in their offices, they had to call traders who were on the floor of the New York Stock Exchange.

Klein thought this was a ridiculous waste of time—the traders were super busy and couldn't always answer the phone—and he invented a "General Associates' Bond Quote Monitor" to allow quotes to funnel direct from the trading floor to the office. He gave the system to a bond trader friend for free and the results were spectacular.

Soon, other bond traders were sniffing around about how the first bond trader was able to receive quotes so quickly and respond to them. Klein was deluged with phone calls and orders for the Monitor.

Try giving your product or service to an influencer for free to prove its value. Then others will be pounding on your door to have it.

> *If you aren't willing to do all of the things that cost money, why should I say "Yes" to investing in your business?*
>
> —Dan Fleyshman, angel investor

WEALTH HACK #56

It's okay to be fashionably late.

Being first to market is not always what it's cracked up to be. Motorola was first in smartphones. Blockbuster was before Netflix. Sears controlled everything before Amazon. Friendster and Myspace were both there before Facebook.

By being second or third, you let everyone else invest all of their money to get recognition for the product category, and you don't have to pay anything. At the same time, you let your competition make all of the mistakes out of the gate—and you can avoid them.

The tortoise was pretty slow, but ultimately he beat the hare in the race. Don't bow out of the competition just because someone else jumped out of the gate first. You can create something infinitely better and smarter.

It's not about being the first to market—it's about being the first to get it right.

—Benny Xian, entrepreneur and founder of Voyadi

WEALTH HACK #57

Remove egos from creative decision-making.

I t goes without saying that business partnerships and collaborations can be challenging. They require a ton of trust—not just in terms of the money matters, but also when it comes to *creative trust*.

In order to survive and thrive, entrepreneurs and business owners need to be aggressive, strong-minded people. They have to be pretty confident that their products, services, and ideas will succeed, no matter what.

At the same time, creative people—designers, graphic artists, and copywriters—can also be pretty strong-minded and proud of their work, as well they should be.

But when it comes to creative decision-making—especially regarding design—sometimes it's hard to know if there is a "right" answer when there is disagreement among different factions.

The key to settling this is that no one's *ego* should be part of the creative decision-making process. It doesn't matter if the founder, designer, or mailroom clerk came up with the best approach. The main thing is that the decision was based on the customer, not on any one person's ego.

Rob Angel was originally a waiter who livened up his party games by randomly choosing a word from the dictionary and drawing it for partiers to guess what it was. Whether he was aware of it or not, he was putting a twist on an old classic: *charades*.

Two years later, he found his old word-prompt notes lying around and decided to expand on the idea. He read through the entire dictionary, found two partners, and self-published it as a game: Pictionary.

When Angel and his team were first producing Pictionary, one of his partners changed the color of the box design to white. The designer was *furious*—not because the color change was the wrong choice, but because it wasn't *his* design color.

In the end, that design won awards and became one of the best-selling entertainment products the world has ever known.

In your business, have a big ego when it comes to banging on doors and selling your wares. But check your ego at the door when making creative decisions.

Never let your ego get so close to your position that when your position goes, your ego goes with it.
                                   —Colin Powell, retired four-star
                                   United States Army general

WEALTH HACK #58

Don't pay retail.

When a store displays the MSRP—the manufacturer's *suggested* retail price—it means just that. It's what the people who made the product *think* the retailer should charge for it.

The shop always pays *way* below that amount.

Example: When a car dealer sells vehicles at "sticker," it means they are doing so at the full retail price. Don't be fooled into thinking they are doing you any favors.

The fact is, until you can get your new wheels for under the sticker price, you are not even beginning to know real value.

Wealthy people know this and ask the one single question that saves them fortunes: "Is that the *best* you can do?"

The price of a car, a dress, a suit, and pretty much everything else is marked up so high, there is almost always a massive amount of wiggle room to negotiate. You'll be surprised at how every cashier and sales representative has the power to lower the price when asked.

Try it.

You will quickly discover that "Is that the *best* you can do?" is the phrase that pays.

Tip: Rich People Love a Good Deal

According to a white paper by University of Michigan researchers A. Yesim Orhun and Mike Palazzolo, wealthy people are far more likely to save money buying in bulk than low-income people. Rich people also purchase more goods on sale than other groups. Millionaires and billionaires know and understand that it's as important to continuously build their fortunes by keeping their controllable spending down.

There is no shame in being a smart shopper! The shame would be in spending more than you need to.

Never pay retail.

—Warren Buffett, investor and chairman
and CEO of Berkshire Hathaway

WEALTH HACK #59

*Don't be afraid to part with
something you love.*

Business owners spend years busting their butts to build their company from the ground up. They bootstrap, scratch, and claw. They make some great business decisions and some whopper mistakes—which they learn from. Eventually, the business takes off and blossoms.

Now that the company has peaked, what's next? Engineer and entrepreneur Dan Smith was in that situation with one of his companies. He had a ton of sweat equity in the business and it had become a huge part of his life. He was sure he would retire with it.

Then things changed: Someone wanted to buy Dan's company. He didn't know what to do. Could he part with something he loved so much? Unlike Jeff Fried who made a *bold move* by choosing to manage a boxer (see Wealth Hack #21) to find his fortune in the first place, Dan was already on the other side of his business. Was it more beneficial to keep the company or sell it? How do you find the emotional courage to separate from your beloved business—something you nurtured from its infancy all the way through adolescence and into maturity?

Dan checked in with his mentor, who told him he should sell it. With some trepidation, he listened to the advice. He took the money from the sale and bought foreclosures, which he flipped at great profit. It gave him a ton of access to capital and opened doors to new revenue streams.

If you are deeply connected to your business and love what you do, that's great. But be open to letting go and freeing yourself up so you can grab something you might eventually love even more.

If you fall in love with the wheelbarrow, you'll spin in circles.

—Anonymous

WEALTH HACK #60

Drive one hammer with one nail.

This is a really simple concept to follow.

If you have one hammer and one nail, you'll get your job done and build something great. If you have two hammers and two nails and pound with both hands at the same time, what do you think is going to happen?

You'll have two bent nails and maybe a busted finger, that's what.

Entrepreneur and keynote speaker Scott Duffy refers to this as the "Hammer and Nails Syndrome." Entrepreneurs tend to focus on too many things at the same time. They think it's great they can multitask and get so much done. But are they really *getting things done well?* Probably not.

Hammer in one nail perfectly and then move on to the next one. As Duffy writes in his book *Launch! The Critical 90 Days from Idea to Market*: "Remember, the best shortcut is taking the long-term view."

Multitasking is a lie.

—Gary W. Keller, entrepreneur and
founder of Keller Williams

WEALTH HACK #61

Clues, patterns, choices.

Move over Austin Powers—Mark Anthony Bates is the real "international man of mystery." A self-proclaimed "solopreneur" and "connector," he travels the globe as a coach to people like Tony Robbins and Richard Branson.

Bates has a philosophy called CPC, which he believes is the secret of all awareness and accountability for success and failure in business.

C = CLUES
P = PATTERNS
C = CHOICES

For example, let's say you have a business meeting and the client shows up late. Well, there's a *clue* that something may be off. The reason he provides for being late may or may not be true—who knows? It's just a *clue*.

The first meeting went well enough to warrant a second one. He ends up being late again. Suddenly the *clue* has turned into a repeated *pattern*.

Now it's up to you to make a *choice* based on this *pattern*: Are you going to continue to do business with him, get upset, or even confront him about it and demand he show greater respect for your time if you are going to work together.

The reality is that you can't and shouldn't attempt to change the person who was late. It's not your responsibility. He is who he is.

Instead, it's your responsibility—your *choice*—about whether you are going to accept the lateness or do business with someone else. This works in all forms of relationships, whether business or personal.

Success leaves clues.
    —Jim Rohn, entrepreneur and motivational speaker

WEALTH HACK #62

Break through constraints.

M any entrepreneurs and salespeople assume that just because a store doesn't carry a certain type of product that it never will. They also make the wrong assumption that a clothing or accessory retailer won't ever stock anything except clothing and accessories.

For years, the Nordstrom department store chain was known primarily for shoes and handbags. They certainly didn't have anything resembling a gaming department in the late 1980s and early 1990s.

But that didn't prevent Rob Angel from pitching his brand-new game to an elite department store. Despite the fact that they didn't carry any games or have a gaming department, they bought 172 units of Pictionary.

What's special about Rob's vision is that he saw everyone and everything as a potential customer for his product—whether it was a yogurt shop or a shoe store, he saw dollar signs others may have overlooked.

Risk Means Reward

If you are an entrepreneur, you are going to need to take a few risks. Some will pay off and some will bomb. These major successes took risks at pivotal times that could have cost them everything:

- Elon Musk: Left PayPal to start SpaceX and Tesla, which are completely outside the dot.com world.
- Bill Gates: Quit college(!) to start Microsoft.
- Dr. Phil: Quit his successful private clinical psychology practice to launch a TV show.
- Robin Chase: Founded Zipcar with only seventy-eight dollars in the bank.
- James Dyson: Created five thousand versions of his vacuum cleaner and went into around $4 million in debt until the final Dyson vacuum was settled on.

Never allow constraints to hold back your business. Your one unusual power move could be the one that opens everything up.

There are no constraints on the human mind, no walls around the human spirit, no barriers to our progress except those we ourselves erect.
—Ronald Reagan, fortieth president of the United States

WEALTH HACK #63

Network outside your industry.

I f you own a liquor store and only hang out with other store owners, all you're going to know is that industry.

If you own a pizza parlor and only pal around with other people who own pizzerias, all you're going to know is the pizza business.

Of course, alcohol and pizza—food and drink—go great together. So why wouldn't the liquor store owner want to hang out with pizza store owners to broaden her community (and vice versa)?

The liquor store owner can give out coupons for 50 percent off a pizza pie to anyone who buys a case of beer. The pizza parlor owner can throw a 50 percent discount coupon for a case of beer inside a pizza box.

The liquor store owner and pizza parlor owner are sharing customers. They are broadening their networks and increasing revenue opportunities by going outside their industries.

Partner up and share contacts with like-minded oddball geniuses such as yourself.

—Anonymous

WEALTH HACK #64

Join a mastermind.

The previous Wealth Hack recommended networking outside your industry. Now we are going to take this concept to a whole new level. The world's most successful people join "mastermind" groups, which is kind of like networking on steroids.

When Elon Musk wanted to get into the car business and involved in space flight, he consulted with the world's greatest minds to turn his dreams into a reality. The cliché is "two heads are better than one"—but imagine what you could accomplish if you have access to three, four, or even eight of the most brilliant minds in your field!

Here's how masterminds work. Reach out to eight business titans in your area. They may or may not be affiliated with your industry or the one you'd like to enter, but that's okay. For example, you might invite the top real estate broker, car dealer, and retailer in your town. Ask if they'd be open to meeting as a group for dinner (or just coffee, drinks, dessert, etc.) on a monthly basis to share their projects, wisdom, and desires with each other.

The Original Mastermind

Who was the originator of the "mastermind" concept? Napoleon Hill, of course.

Many people presume he created the concept in *Think and Grow Rich*, but he actually first introduced it in *The Law of Success*, which was introduced in limited edition in 1925 and fully published in 1928. It's been called different things over the years—"mastermind alliance" and now "mastermind group," but the idea is still pretty much the same and stands the test of time.

At the first session, after everyone is comfortable and has gotten to know each other, create a simple group vision statement. Your unified purpose—however you would like to state it—is to help each other grow their businesses, problem solve, share important contacts, and improve the community.

In time, you'll find that your mastermind group has opened you up to all kinds of opportunities and ideas you otherwise would not have considered. They are there for you in the same way you are there for them.

Someday, many years from now when you are at the same level as Elon Musk, you will be asked to join the mastermind group of a budding young entrepreneur—and you will happily accept the invitation.

No two minds ever come together without, thereby, creating a third, invisible, intangible force which may be likened to a third mind.

    —Napoleon Hill, author of *Think and Grow Rich*

WEALTH HACK #65

Pivot!

Sometimes in business you think you're doing everything right, yet nothing seems to work.

Years ago, Brian Smith—the founder of UGG boots—created a product line of footwear for the beach. The natural thing was to hire sexy models surfing on the beach to advertise the product.

The campaign bombed. Smith couldn't understand how advertising with beautiful surfer models could possibly fail. He probed his customers and found out something important: *The models didn't look like they could surf.* They were totally unconvincing and wrong for the audience.

Smith had to do a complete reversal and find models who surfed, to lend credibility to the campaign. Once his company changed direction, the advertising strategy suddenly started to click.

Your customers tell you the direction in which you need to pivot. Follow them.

Strap On Your Boots!
Boots may evolve and adapt with the styles and trends of the time, but they never go away. In addition to UGG, there are many brands competing for your feet: Red Wing Shoes, Timberland, Dr. Martens, the Frye Company, Wolverine, and many others. Create a fresh boot design for an untapped or rising consumer group, and you might be stepping into a gold mine.

There is only one boss. The customer.
—Sam Walton, founder of Walmart and Sam's Club

WEALTH HACK #66

Crush up your vitamins.

Harry S. Truman said, "Not all readers are leaders, but all leaders are readers."

Here's a saying for today: "Information absorbers are the billionaires of tomorrow."

Back in the "old days," most billionaires were voracious readers. They had ginormous libraries with built-in bookcases and read a book a day.

This may come as something of a shock to you. The Wealth Hackers who contributed to this book aren't avid book readers. Some of them have *written and published* books and have read a few over the years, but they are not literary mavens in the same way as billionaires of the past.

That doesn't mean billionaires don't read. They certainly do—and they soak up *everything*.

Today's cash-rich titans do things differently. They immerse themselves in blogs, trending social media posts, audiobooks, videos, podcasts, and in-person exchanges more so than from traditional "books." Their never-ending education is evolving with the digital era. They prefer the interactivity and multiple dimensions of other formats—plus, usually these other sources and formats are a lot shorter and faster. YouTube videos are taking up everyone's mindshare and guiding the future.

We're all pressed for time, right?

Let's not hate on books. We love them, right? You're reading one right now! Books may not have the same real-time flair as cutting-edge digital formats, but they have the benefit of editorial scrutiny and dig much deeper into topics than any blog possibly could.

Great literature will always stand the test of time. *So: If you love to read bound copies, keep reading them!*

The point is this: *Absorbing content is like taking vitamins.* It doesn't matter if you crush them, drink them, eat chewables, or swallow tablets. The result is the same.

By reading and processing a wealth of content in a variety of formats—especially the one that works for you—you're still getting food and energy for your brain.

Content is king.
—Bill Gates, principal founder of Microsoft Corporation

WEALTH HACK #67

Answer the phone.

The most successful people are those who are most available and willing to share their contacts and knowledge. The Wealth Hackers included in this book either appeared at my events and/or answered my phone calls to schedule in-person interviews. Not a single one of them ignored my query or shut me down—even if they'd never heard of me before we spoke. I just picked up the phone, dialed, and they answered. I now consider them to be part of my network and I count most of them among my friends. They answer my calls and I *always* do the same when they reach out to me.

Emblazon this in your mind: wealthy people respond to texts, emails, messenger inquiries, social media posts, and phone messages. They *engage*.

We're flooded by communication 24/7 in so many ways, but today more than ever people seem suspicious of outreach and tune out more than they tune in.

Everyone else deserves a chance. You never know when an unlikely connection can lead to a major business lead. Or how gratifying it can be to spend a few minutes helping someone else out with expert advice.

Your time is valuable and does need to be monitored. But don't block out every communication just because you don't (yet) personally know the individual. If it's not spam or an unwanted sales pitch, pick up the phone.

Make the Call NOW

Eighty percent of every single thing we need is already within our sphere of influence. The objects are right there in front of us: the business card on our desk, the contact on our cell phone waiting for the perfect time to call.

Unfortunately, most of us are held back by the "once I"s:

I'll make the call **once I** *get the kids out the house.*
I'll send the email **once I** *feel worthy.*

In fact, the best time to take action is now.

Take this challenge today: Open up your phone and call the person you fear the most and have put off contacting. You'll be amazed by how eager he or she is to hear from you.

Get closer to the people you can impact.

—Sharon Lechter, accountant, motivational
speaker, and philanthropist

WEALTH HACK #68

Pay yourself first.

Wealthy people understand the importance of paying your-self before anyone else.

Every time you receive a check, you need to write one to yourself. The future of your business depends on it.

Not only does "paying yourself first" mean putting enough money in your personal accounts, it also means taking enough of a cut of your regular earnings for an emergency fund and your retirement accounts. It also determines how wealthy you will become.

Most people take their paychecks and automatically spend money on cars, clothing, travel, and other luxury items. They figure they'll save the money "later." What they don't realize is that they are missing out on all of that *compound growth*—a constant amount of money made over a period of time.

If you pay yourself first and squirrel away little bits at a time as a habit, you'll receive long-term results without having to do anything. Employees are obviously critical and must be paid right after, or you risk losing good people. If you are so strapped that you truly can't save money for a period of time, keep tabs on those lean weeks and add that extra amount back in when you are on track and have a surplus of cash.

Otherwise, no matter how painful it might feel, heed this advice: At the end of each month, when you're facing a stack of bills and have your checkbook out, always write the very first check payable to yourself.

Fill your cup first. Feed the world with what flows over.
—Les Brown, legendary motivational speaker

WEALTH HACK #69

Create a euphoric sense of contribution.

Many entrepreneurs believe the key to success is *money, money, money*. This perception couldn't be truer than in the financial sector.

But there's one financial advisor, Jeff Levitan, whose purpose is all about charity. He has worked tirelessly to combat childhood poverty on both the local and international levels.

When it comes to handling clients, most would prefer to work with someone who is a "good guy." Like the old adage goes: "Find a way to do well by doing good."

Contrary to popular belief, many of the world's richest people are not misers when it comes to giving back. Every year, billionaires such as Bill Gates, George Soros, Warren Buffett, and Michael Bloomberg give away billions of dollars to various charities.

People want to work with businesses that give back. They want to work with a specific person, not just a corporate entity. They will spend more on a cause than on only making money. Most of all, in the financial arena, they are looking for people who they trust to handle money—people who are authentic in their humanitarian efforts.

What causes do you support? What charity do you whole-heartedly believe in that you can connect with your business?

It doesn't take a lot of money to get involved in charitable causes. Donate what you can afford and increase the amounts as your business expands.

Bounty always receives value from the manner in which it is bestowed.

—Samuel Johnson, poet, essayist,
lexicographer, and philanthropist

WEALTH HACK #70

Make your money work for you.

You've probably heard the cliché: *Have your money work for you, instead of working for your money.*

But what does this really mean? Every financial advisor and expert seems to have a different answer, so let's simplify it.

If you're just collecting a paycheck, paying bills, and spending what's leftover on wants as well as needs, you are not giving your money a chance to work for you. The goal is to find ways to *build assets through income.*

The gumball machine mentioned in Wealth Hack #54 is one variant example of this type of revenue stream. Here's another: Invest in a rental property. The rent you receive covers your home mortgage with a little over the top to spare. That little bit of extra income is making money for you each month without you having to do a thing.

Sometimes Passive Is Positive

Passive income is also sometimes known as "mailbox money." Who doesn't love that thrill of reaching into the mailbox, pulling out an envelope, and finding a check inside? Of course, direct deposit, PayPal, and other electronic transfer methods exist today, but the idea of "found money" is still implied by the "mailbox" concept.

There are many ways to receive unexpected income. Any business that has a membership component (i.e., continuity) receives regular (monthly, quarterly, or annual) payments. You could start a website or build an online course. If you happen to have an extra room in your apartment or house, you might be able to rent it out for regular monthly income.

Wherever possible, try to find multiple passive revenue streams to keep your mailbox full. The graphic below illustrates the point of how to build wealth through continuity/mailbox money.

HOW TO MAKE
$1,000,000

SELL A $200 PRODUCT TO 5,000 PEOPLE.
SELL A $500 PRODUCT TO 2,000 PEOPLE.
SELL A $1,000 PRODUCT TO 1,000 PEOPLE.
SELL A $2,000 PRODUCT TO 500 PEOPLE.
SELL A $4,000 PRODUCT TO 250 PEOPLE.

OR:

5,000 PEOPLE PAY $17 PER MONTH FOR 12 MONTHS.
2,000 PEOPLE PAY $42 PER MONTH FOR 12 MONTHS.
1,000 PEOPLE PAY $83 PER MONTH FOR 12 MONTHS.
500 PEOPLE PAY $167 PER MONTH FOR 12 MONTHS.
250 PEOPLE PAY $333 PER MONTH FOR 12 MONTHS.

Too many people spend money they earned . . . to buy things they don't want . . . to impress people that they don't like.

—Will Rogers, actor, humorist, and social commentator

WEALTH HACK #71

*Do the opposite of what
everyone tells you to do.*

D an Smith, a pioneer in the oil and gas industries and president of the Energy Capital Fund, is not afraid to take risks and do the exact opposite of what everyone else is doing.

"I'm always open to new ideas," he says. "If they fail, I'm rewarded by simply having tried."

While Dan worked at XTO Energy in the 1990s, he played a key role in the technological revolution of hydraulic fracturing. (Yes, this process is a type of *fracking*—i.e., using force to open up fissures in order to extract oil or gas. This Wealth Hack does not condone or condemn this controversial process believed to be harmful to the environment. It merely happens to be the example.) This development helped unlock tremendous reserves of oil and gas in the United States.

At first, people cautioned him that the process would never work and that it was waste of time, money, and resources. Everyone told him it was crazy. But Dan said, "Let's try it," and the gamble paid off. Not only did it succeed at the same level as the prior method, but it also cost one-tenth the amount.

Sometimes doing the opposite of what everyone tells you to do—or *not* do—pays off much bigger than sticking with the status quo.

If everybody is doing it one way, there's a good chance you can find your niche by going exactly in the opposite direction.

—Sam Walton, founder of Walmart and Sam's Club

WEALTH HACK #72

Decide whether you want fame or fortune.

Y ou can start out wanting to be famous. Or you can start out wanting to get rich.

According to TV host, C-Suite consultant, and best-selling author Jeffrey Hayzlett, you can't pursue both. You must choose.

The odds are stacked against becoming rich and famous at the same time. Only a select few (think Paris Hilton) are able to accomplish this, and you need a lot of luck, connections, and exceptional timing to make it happen.

Dig deep and focus seriously on this question—*fame or fortune*—and then decide on one or the other. If you strive toward achieving fame, the riches will come later. If you become rich, you can channel that wealth to become famous.

Fame and fortune are as hard to find as a lightning strike.
—P. N. Elrod, novelist

WEALTH HACK #73

Debunk the relationship myth.

You probably think billionaires like to fool around only with glamorous, gorgeous people and ultimately choose to settle down with fancy trophy spouses.

Not true: *It's a myth.*

Nearly all of the leaders interviewed for this book—Brian Sidorsky and Ron Klein immediately come to mind—have maintained long-term relationships with *equal partners who have been amazing confidants and support anchors.*

This is a powerful common denominator among many super-wealthy people: They have spouses who stayed with them through thick and thin and became the sounding boards behind many of their major ideas and greatest accomplishments.

Love and Marriage Create Happiness and Wealth

While it's not true that every single billionaire has had loving, long-term relationships—there are notable exceptions—it's remarkable to rattle off the names of those who have been able to sustain their marriages for many years. These are just a few who remained together for well over two decades:

- Bill and Melinda Gates (still married)
- Paul and Linda McCartney (married twenty-nine years until her death in 1998)
- Carlos Slim and Soumaya Domit (married thirty-two years until her death in 1999)
- Warren and Susan Buffett (married fifty-two years until her death in 2004)
- Jeff and MacKenzie Bezos (still married)
- Eric and Wendy Schmidt (still married)
- Phil and Penelope Knight (still married)
- Richard Branson and Joan Templeman (still married)

Even in politics, many of the world's most powerful people have enduring marriages. To name a few: *George Washington had Martha. Abe Lincoln had Mary Todd. Franklin Delano Roosevelt had Eleanor. Winston Churchill had Clementine. Ronald Reagan had Nancy. George Bush had Barbara. G. W. Bush has Laura. Barack Obama has Michelle.*

Think about it.

The cliché that you "can't choose your family" is simply not true. You *do* have control over selecting the person with whom you'll spend your entire life. From a spouse comes children, grandchildren, and so on—all of whom originated from the person you made a conscious decision to spend your life with.

Choose your life partner wisely.

> *Behind every great man is a woman. Telling him he's not so hot.*
>
> —Harrison Ford, actor

WEALTH HACK #74

*The true difference between
the rich and the wealthy.*

You could be rich—even a millionaire—but you'll never be able to afford an NFL team. You might own the greatest car dealership in your town or community, but chances are you'll never be able to buy NASCAR.

With that mind, what if we were to tell you that this final Wealth Hack is completely opposite the other 73 that come before it?

When a certain billionaire was asked by the author why he was so successful when so many others were not, his reply was staggering: "Because others believe the bullshit lies they are told and sold on TV."

Looking at the author square in the eye, he said, "People read those motivational feel-good books, buy the misleading programs they see on late-night infomercials, and listen to the mass messaging rather than following the proven actions of the wealthy."

Stunned, the author asked, "What is the biggest lie?"

"That's easy," replied the suited gentleman. "Follow your passion and the money will follow."

The author was dumbfounded. This goes against pretty much all the advice of success books over the last fifty years. "What are you talking about?" the author demanded.

"That is what we have heard for our entire lives, there is even a famous quote—sometimes attributed to either Confucius or Mark Twain—that says, 'When you love what you do, you'll never work a day in your life.'"

The billionaire leaned in and whispered, "Hogwash."

Again the author pressed for clarity: "Can you explain?"

"As you know, around 85 percent of all new businesses fail each year—sure, you've heard the statistics a thousand times." Jokingly he added, "Did you know that 74.7 percent of all statistics are made up?"

The author grinned as the wealthy man continued: "The reason they fail is *not* lack of funding, lack of viability, or anything of the sort. It's due to the lie that I just mentioned . . .

"Imagine a guy working as welder. He gives his entire life towards his craft to finally save a few dollars. He hears the age-old cliché, follows his passion, and uses those funds to quit his career and open a yogurt shop because he really likes yogurt. Now, this guy knows *nothing* about yogurt, let alone has the business acumen to begin a new business. Yet, like so many others, he listened to a few motivational programs, read the latest self-help books, and is all fired up to go live his destiny in the yogurt empire. In other words, he's following his passion."

"How can you be so sure starting his own yogurt business is the wrong thing for him to do? Maybe his passion will enable him to learn."

"Nothing is wrong with starting a business, that's the easy part. It's keeping it going is where the challenge lies. Remember, 85 percent fail their first year and, among those who survive, 50 percent close the following year."

"Why?"

"Because it's their passion. You see, they treat their business like it's their baby. It takes over their lives."

"What is wrong with that?" the author asked.

"Because they treat it like their child rather than a business. They hold on to bad employees too long—or make decisions based on *feelings* rather than on good business practice. They become captain of the ship and go down with the boat while drowning everyone and everything left on board."

The author's eyes widened at the visual.

"I see myself as the character in a video game," he said. "I ride one log coasting along the stream until it begins going under, then I jump off to the next log floating by and ride that one for its journey. I'll never go down because I'll never become emotionally attached to any one entity. I treat my business like a *business*, not like my baby."

The student asked, "So passion never comes into play?"

"Yes, of course, that's the best part. Passion is what drives us and fuels the engine to get us started and excited in the first place. It's also comes into play once we capitalize on the opportunities and build wealth. We *use* that wealth to finance our passion. Most people do this in reverse. This is why so few ever feel like they have really made a mark on this spinning rock."

"There must be *some* people who followed their passion towards wealth," the author offered.

"Of course, there are examples—but understand this. You can get rich following your passion, and make millions absolutely; however, you'll never know *massive wealth* following this philosophy. Do you really think the Rockefellers were passionate about the monetary system? Or the Gettys woke up excited about crude oil? Or people who made fortunes in waste management were following their hearts towards garbage? Or the people who paved the roads and built our bridges were emotionally connected to sand? They seized opportunity.

"In turn, they used that prosperity to help create the amazing country we know today. The fact is, the people who capitalize on their opportunity to create the greatest wealth are also the individuals who started nearly every major university the world has ever known. In addition, they financed fine arts, such as ballet and museums, and currently even back our most fun leisure activities, such as professional sports and entertainment.

"Tell me: Do you honestly believe that the sheiks of the Arabic states walk the oil fields in awe of the liquid that lies beneath their feet?"

Mesmerized by the realization, the author was forced to reconsider everything he once thought true.

The emotions associated with passion can get in the way of building and maintaining a business that leads to a massive fortune.

Where we have strong emotions, we're liable to fool ourselves.
    —Carl Sagan, astronomer and science communicator

PARTING WORDS

*R*iches begin with thought.

Those words from Napoleon Hill in *Think and Grow Rich* remain timeless and universal.

If there is one common denominator among all the Wealth Hackers included in this work, it's that *faith, desire, imagination,* and *persistence* continue to be lasting and proven attributes among the super wealthy.

From the Henry Fords and Andrew Carnegies of the past to the Ron Kleins and Tonino Lamborghinis of today, *riches begin in the form of thought.*

Believe.

Conquer fear.

Never stop because someone says "no."

Convince yourself that you deserve abundance.

Da Vinci, Franklin, Edison, Marconi, the Wright Brothers, Gates, Buffett, Jobs, and Winfrey have nothing on you. Your dreams are even grander. As Napoleon Hill wrote, "The world is filled with an abundance of opportunity that the dreamers of the past never knew."

Are you ready? It's time to put down this book and *take action*. Put into practice as many gold nuggets in this book as possible. *Do them now!*

ACKNOWLEDGMENTS

First, a big shout out to Brian Sidorsky, whose germ of an idea became the foundation for this book.

The author (Dr. Greg Reid, that is) would like to extend his deepest thanks to all of the brilliant Wealth Hackers who allowed the coauthor (Gary Krebs) and me to probe their minds and sift out their best, most effective gold nuggets.

In particular, I am deeply appreciative of those individuals who devoted their valuable time for private one-on-one interviews: Kevin Harrington; Tonino Lamborghini; Craig Shah; Dan Smith; Marc Staniloff; Reed Knight, Jr.; Jeffrey Hayzlett; and Jeff Levitan.

Special thanks and appreciation goes out to our personal Mastermind Association that accepted the challenge to join us along this mission:

Scott Utterback

Simon Lovell

James Blakemore

Clarissa Burt

Kevin Gordon

Joshua Earp

John Chase

William Anthony Dean

Krysten Maracle

Frank Karako

Eric Osche

Brian Tweer

I also would like to single out Katrina Thornton, Katiana Sanchez, and Theo Davies, who did so much to help this book from behind the scenes.

My agent, Bill Gladstone at Waterside Productions, has been an outstanding resource and staunch supporter. I appreciate everything you do, my friend.

The folks at BenBella have been amazing: Thank you Glenn Yeffeth, Adrienne Lang, Sarah (Dombrowsky) Avinger, Alexa Stevenson, and Scott Calamar.

Lastly, this book would not have been possible without the support and invaluable suggestions of attendees of my Secret Knock and Prosperity Camp events. You guys ROCK!

About the Authors

Dr. Greg Reid, who received his honorary PhD in Literature, has been named one of the top five keynote speakers by *Forbes* and *Entrepreneur*. He has been published in more than 70 books, which have been translated into 45 languages. Among his bestselling titles are *Stickability* and *Three Feet from Gold*.

A successful entrepreneur known for his giving spirit, Dr. Reid has a knack for translating complicated situations into simple, digestible concepts. As an action-taking phenomenon, his strategy turns into fast and furious results. His relationships are deep and rich in the space he orbits, and he is a firm believer in the role of win-win partnerships and making a difference to others in order to succeed.

He can be found having a great time brewing up inspiration, occasionally breaking into song and dance, and being of contribution to those around him.

Gary M. Krebs, founder of GMK Writing and Editing, Inc., is a writer, literary agent, and longtime business book publisher at Brilliance Publishing (Amazon Publishing), McGraw-Hill Professional, Globe Pequot Press, Adams Media, and Macmillan. He was also US Editor of *The Guinness Book of Records*. His works include *Creating Sales Stars* (with Stephan Schiffman) and *The Rock and Roll Reader's Guide*. Mr. Krebs, who received his BFA from the Dramatic Writing Program, Tisch School of the Arts (NYU), resides in Fairfield, CT.